Circles in Stone

A BRITISH PREHISTORIC MYSTERY

I dedicate this book to Irene and Ian Hewitt, my co-Directors in the excavation of the Blawearie Cairns (1984-8), who have for years been my close friends, helped me in my research, and have done their best to improve my recording system.

Those who are not content unless every mystery is fully explained may feel dissatisfied, that after all the labour research bestowed on the inscribed rocks, we cannot read them off as from a lettered book. ...Something, however, has been achieved – materials for aiding in the fuller solution of the problem have been placed on record – an advanced starting point made for future enquiries – and a description and representation preserved of marvellous sculptures which time and the elements will eventually obliterate.

George Tate, Alnwick historian, *1865*

Circles in Stone
A BRITISH PREHISTORIC MYSTERY

Stan Beckensall

TEMPUS

First published 2006

Tempus Publishing Limited
The Mill, Brimscombe Port,
Stroud, Gloucestershire, GL5 2QG
www.tempus-publishing.com

British Library Cataloguing in Publication Data.
A catalogue record for this book is available from the British Library.

ISBN 0 7524 4015 2

Typesetting and origination by Tempus Publishing Limited
Printed in Great Britain

Contents

Foreword

At some point after 6000 years ago a Neolithic person picked up a hard stone tool and started pecking away on softer rock to make the first open-air carving in Britain. We have no idea what thoughts and feelings moved this person to create this inscription, but we do know that this act initiated a carving tradition in Britain that lasted for about 2000 years until the Early Bronze Age and witnessed many thousands of rocks being decorated with abstract motifs consisting primarily of cups and grooves. Found mainly in northern Britain, these inscribed rocks vary in size from the massive outcrop rock at Achnabreck in Scotland to small single-cupped portables that can be held in one hand.

Being such a marked feature of the landscape, it is likely that many of our ancestors would have been aware of these inscribed rocks and had their own stories about their origin and meaning. None of these have survived in oral testimonies or in early writings, which is unfortunate because it would be very satisfying to know, for example, what the Iron Age people who incorporated some of these carved boulders into their hillfort structures thought about them. These enigmatic carved rocks first entered our modern historical consciousness in the last several hundred years when early antiquarians and learned clergyman began to take an interest in ancient things that survived in the landscape. To begin with, not all were convinced of the antiquity of the decorated rocks. It was only after he found his second carved rock at Old Bewick that John Langlands, who is credited with being the discoverer of ancient rock carvings in Northumberland (in the 1820s), was convinced that they weren't simply the work of shepherds.

After accepting the carvings as being ancient, the Victorians set out to discover and record them with gusto. Prominent among these were the Alnwick antiquarian George Tate and eminent Scottish physician Sir James Simpson, who produced the first rock-art gazetteers in the 1860s. Following the heady days of rock-art activity of the mid and late nineteenth century there was a lull in their recording until the second half of the twentieth century, when the study was revived by rock-art enthusiasts who have done much excellent work without the benefit of institutional support. Many people have contributed to this (e.g. Keith Boughey and Ed Vickerman and the Ilkley Archaeology Group, Tim Laurie and Maarten van Hoek), but the two individuals with whom this rock-art revival is chiefly associated are the late Ronald Morris and Stan Beckensall. The connection between these two rock-art researchers was cemented when Ronald Morris bequeathed to Stan his Nikon camera (which Stan still proudly uses) and his Scottish archive, which Stan has now returned to Scotland.

Stan's interest in rock-art was inspired by an encounter in the mid-1960s with the same large, elaborately decorated, rock at Old Bewick which had captured Langlands' imagination some 140 years previously. On his discovery Stan commented that:

> Long before I found these words of Mr Tate [describing the Langlands discovery], by strange coincidence my interest in northern rock carvings began at the very same place. I remember clearly a day of mist and drizzle, when my daughter, niece and I saw the large stone at Old Bewick for the first time. Not long before, my family had been living in Malta's sunshine, where the stone carvings had been of a different nature. Yet here was a link – the urge that prehistoric people had to incise or peck the symbols of their religion onto rock. Hundreds of miles separated the two places, but the intention, and perhaps the inspiration, was similar. (Beckensall 1984:9)

Initially Stan's recording efforts were concentrated in his adopted home county of Northumberland, where following in the footsteps of George Tate – literally and figuratively – he vigorously recorded as many carved rocks as he was able to while still keeping his day job as an educator and Head Teacher. In the 1980s and the early 1990s Stan was joined by Ian and Irene Hewitt – to whom this book is dedicated – who helped him to streamline his recording system. It was also during this time that he refined his rubbing and redrawing techniques. With early retirement in the early 1990s came the freedom to expand his horizon and explore the prehistoric carvings of other places in greater detail and to engage with rock-art researchers in these areas. Publications ensued not only on Northumberland but also on County Durham, Swaledale and Wensleydale (with Tim Laurie), Cumbria and most recently Kilmartin. It was also during this time that Stan's field recordings and publications started to be used by an increasing number of university and institutionally-based rock-art researchers that began to engage with British rock-art. More recently his Northumberland rock-art archive has formed the basis of what is believed to be the largest regional rock-art website in the world.

Stan's desire to share his findings with as large an audience as possible has seen him, during the last 40 years, do an enormous amount to make this subject matter accessible to the public and to actively encourage its enjoyment and further study. I doubt whether there are many people who have given as many slideshows in rural parish halls as Stan and, in doing so, have inspired young and old about ancient Britain! But it is probably through his popular and well-used books that Stan has reached his largest audiences, and it is not unusual to come across rock-art enthusiasts in rural Northumberland clutching one of his publications to assist them in locating and in deciphering panels with his drawings and eloquent commentary.

But *Circles in Stone* is not a regional gazetteer. It is an overview that covers the whole of Britain. In crafting this book Stan has not only drawn on his considerable experience and insights into British rock-art, but he also updates the reader on current thinking in rock-art studies. Stan highlights regional patterns, draws attention to key carved sites and panels, and brings to the reader his interpretations and his views on the recording, conservation, and display of these heritage resources, as well as the need for further research. As is to be expected, this book is generously illustrated with high-quality photographs and drawings, adding enormously to our visual appreciation of the carvings. The book is also richly imbued with stories about many of the people connected to the discovery and recording of the carvings, recognising the contribution that they have made to its study. In bringing together these different strands of British rock-art endeavours and sharing his knowledge and perspectives, Stan has, with this book, made another significant contribution to the study of these enigmatic ancient carvings and, more significantly, to their understanding and appreciation by the general public eager to learn more about the achievements of our distant ancestors.

Aron Mazel
University of Newcastle upon Tyne
June 2006

REFERENCE

Beckensall, S. 1984. Northumberland's Prehistoric Rock Carvings. Rothbury: Pendulum Publications.

Acknowledgements

There are many people to whom I owe a great deal. Many of them are mentioned in the text: those whose work has contributed so much to our knowledge of rock-art.

I thank those who have contributed to photographs and images in this book or have allowed me to use those resulting from my research, such as the National Museums of Scotland and the Royal Commission on the Ancient Monuments of Scotland (especially Jack Stevenson, Alex Hale and John Sherriff). I have also drawn on other people's illustrations, among them Maarten van Hoek, Avril Purcell and Paul Brown. I thank Maureen Lazzari for her excellent maps.

Gerry Bracken introduced me to old and new sites in west Ireland, and arranged for me to share my work with the people of County Mayo.

I have worked closely with Irene and Ian Hewitt, to whom this book is dedicated, and with Paul and Barbara Brown, whose fieldwork is outstanding, and we all remain great friends.

Professors Richard Bradley and John Coles have watched over my work and inspired me and I have been most fortunate in my contact with such people as Drs Aron Mazel, Clive Waddington, Paul Bahn and Paul Frodsham. This makes it read like a who's who in rock-art. They, and Matthew Hutchinson and Jonathan Nicholas have read parts or the entire book and given advice that I have taken.

A particular thank-you is due to many who have reported sites to me, and those who encourage others on the Internet, but I give special thanks to the most recent of these explorers, George Currie, who has had a profound effect on our database for Scotland.

For the future, there are many projects in operation, and I hope that all those who are being encouraged to join in such community projects as the Coquet Valley Project in Northumberland and the English Heritage project for recording Northumberland and Durham, will become the great researchers of tomorrow. Finally, I thank Sharon Simpson for bringing me into her project at Greenfield Community School, and for allowing me to use the outstanding images of the young people's work; a reminder that rock-art has been, and is, by and for everyone.

A link with this work is seen in the design of the cover of this book by Gordon Highmoor, whose art work for all my covers has been unique, and I thank him profoundly for this. He sees rock-art as an integral significant force in the landscape, in special places. He is a climber and archaeologist as well as being an ex-Senior Lecturer in Visual Communication – disciplines which have helped him to invoke landscape rather than merely describe it. He has added a tremendous dimension to the subject.

A note from the author

This book is the result of decades of work. In covering such a wide area it is difficult to know just how much detail to include, for it is intended as an overview rather than a gazetteer. There must, however, be sufficient examples to support generalisations. I have tried to include, particularly, areas that have only been recently discovered, some previously unpublished, perhaps unknown to most readers, and some that have been reassessed. These join the 'classic' sites as part of the thesis.

The work cannot be solitary, and has drawn on the work of others from the beginning of the study of rock-art, and no matter how far we have progressed in our knowledge and understanding, we owe the past everything.

I have tried to give specific references to sites within the text, but have tried not to interrupt the reading with too many parentheses. All fine details of sites are contained in a bibliography and index. I have found it useful to use these abbreviations for general areas in part of the text: Cumbria C, Durham D, Galloway G, Ireland I, Kilmartin K, Northumberland N, North Yorkshire Moors NYM, Peak District P, and West Yorkshire WY. Grid references to sites are included in the index.

It will not be long before someone will want to rewrite this book, as work in rock-art progresses at a fast pace. That is all to the good.

1 Principal areas of rock-art in Scotland, England and Wales. Main concentrations are in heavier type. *Maureen Lazzari*

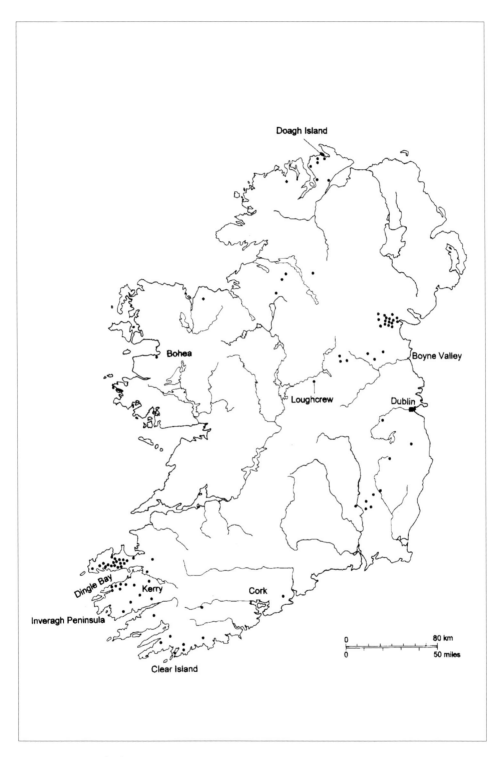

Doagh Island

Bohea

Boyne Valley

Loughcrew

Dublin

Dingle Bay
Kerry
Cork

Inveragh Peninsula

Clear Island

0   80 km
0   50 miles

2 Main sites in Ireland. *Maureen Lazzari*

15

1

Setting the scene:
Strath Tay

It is mid-November in 2005, a clear bright day with blue sky, and I am standing high above Loch Tay on the north side. Far below and to the east are trees, but all around and behind is rough grass and a scatter of a few boulders and the tops of some outcrops of rock. From here many springs rise, and to get to this spot I have had to climb high and steeply, then cross a small ravine through which water rushes at great speed, forming waterfalls in places, to feed the long loch. There is no habitation here, but higher up the slope are abandoned shielings, temporary herds' summer quarters. There are rocks marked with motifs, not at all prominent, but as you stand by each one you have a breath-taking view of a fabulous landscape of water, fields and forest giving way to waste at the higher ground to the south, where hills rise above hills. The land around these rocks appears bare of any traces of human occupation, yet the late autumn sun, low and oblique, illuminates patterns of concentric rings or simple cup-marks that have been overlooked until a recent survey by the Royal Commission on the Ancient and Historical Monuments of Scotland (RCAHMS). They are part of a discovery that extends in patches along the whole ridge westward, multiplying the number of sites significantly, joining those already marked on OS maps at a lower level, including those recorded but now lost, for rock-art is a fragile heritage easily destroyed by farming and quarrying (*colour plate 1*).

One outcrop, a rounded rise, has only a few simple cups: circular, shallow indentations so easy to miss.

Nearby is another outcrop with some quartz forming part of its surface, and squeezed into a suitable space is a series of concentric rings around a cup from which a groove runs to the rock's edge. In less favourable light, water would bring out the pattern. It is tempting to try to align these motifs with a peak across the water, but one soon realizes that this is not necessarily what the makers did. One can also look at the direction of the groove running from the central cup to see what it might point at, but this too is subjective (Rock 1).

Left: 3 Loch Tay panorama south from rock 1

Below and opposite: 4, 5 Rock 1, Ben Lawers

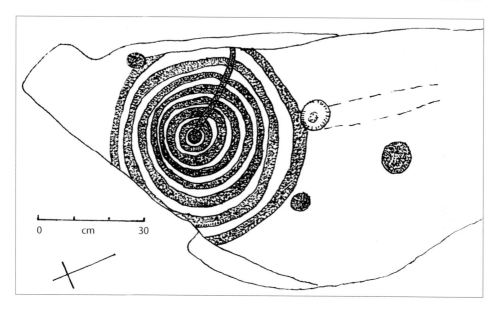

I move closer to the ridge's edge, where there is a remarkable creation carved into the surface of an orange-coloured rock, now darker than when it was first found, that may be an earthfast boulder or outcrop. I marvel that this rock has perhaps not been seen for thousands of years, as far as I know, for no one recorded it until recently. We call patterns like this 'rock-art', and indeed this is art, for to us it gives aesthetic pleasure as a design that takes into account the subtle natural features of the rock surface and fills it. The concentric circles have long been known quite simply as 'cups-and-rings' and I am happy to keep that terminology.

Look closer now. What is going on? How was the pattern achieved? That is one of the easiest questions to answer, as our eyes show us that the grooves and cup are made with some sort of pick. The pecking could have been made with a metal punch, but we are later to learn from other rocks and sources that it was done with a stone pick harder than the parent rock, and impacted either as a hand-held tool or with some kind of mallet (*colour plate 1*, Rock 2).

I had drawn these rocks over a year before this visit and you can now see the results. They took hours of work at the site and at home, and are supported by prints, digital pictures and slides that include the location.

All the rocks in this region have been plotted with a GPS system, which uses satellite technology to locate their places on the earth's surface. From their distribution on maps people try to work out why they are in these positions, to find a logical explanation for their distribution. It is clear from even the limited pictures of three decorated rock surfaces that cups and grooves are used in different ways to produce different results: simple cups through to complex

Above and below: 6, 7 Rock 2, Ben Lawers

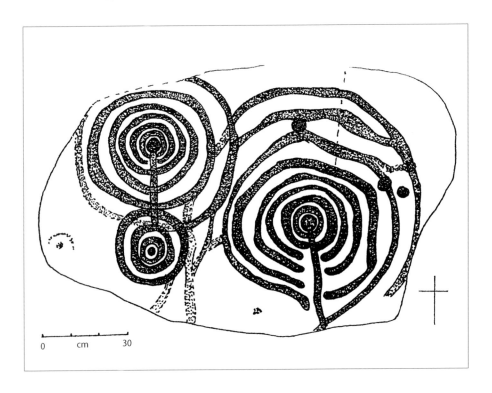

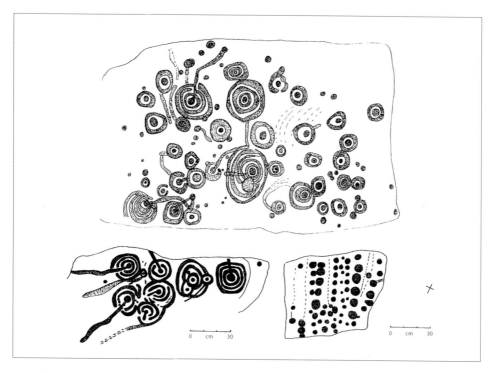

8 Rocks 3, 4 and 5, Ben Lawers

designs. Do they signify different things? Did different people make them? Were they all made at the same time? What on earth were they for?

My companion on this occasion is Paul Frodsham, archaeologist with the Northumberland National Park, who shares my passion for trying to answer such questions. He is one of many professional archaeologists who have entered this field recently, whereas I have been recording the phenomenon all over Britain in my spare time for over 40 years. The main discoveries have been made by non-professionals (i.e. not paid for it), but their accumulation of a huge body of information has provided the means for others to study it, often away from the rocks themselves in offices and laboratories, all bringing new ideas. The study of rock-art has been considerably enriched by a combination of enthusiastic fieldworkers and academics.

Before I show you the work of the latest non-professional fieldworker, let me give you some more examples further west along this ridge. Behind us is the summit of Ben Lawers, which gives the sites their name. They provide further examples of how the motif-makers manipulated simple symbols (cups and grooves) to produce different effects.

One is on a table-sized block rising above the landscape, as tall as a person. Lower down towards the loch, where farming has had a considerable effect on what the landscape looks like, is a stone at the base of a destroyed wall, covered with cups in lines, with no rings.

Finally there is a complex flow of eroded motifs on outcrop at a lower level among other patches of outcrop where no other art is visible.

We have been looking at some examples from among over 120 recently identified by the Royal Commission, spread out parallel to the loch on a foreshore up to 200m high, some on a terrace between 200-400m, and the rest on the treeless open moorland over 400m high.

On the previous day in very different conditions we visited sites to the south of Loch Tay over the hills that rise from the loch to the south-east, all recently discovered by George Currie. George was a member of a Top of the Pops group, 'Darts', and now lives with his wife and son at Tealing, north of Dundee. He caught the rock-art bug when he made important discoveries around the place where he lives, and then pushed further afield, including this part of Perthshire. He contacted me for help with the recording, in the summer of 2005, and I was more than happy to do this, especially as he had discovered a completely new area between two known sites to the east and west. I went there in November to record his latest discovery, which I offer here. Craig Hill gives its name to these sites.

The illustrated panel is the most westerly of his discoveries; plots of the rest are mainly confined to the 465m contour and the 440m one, so they occupy intermediate land between high hills and low, marshy ground. We cannot assume that the vegetation has always looked like this, or that today's climate was the same as it was thousands of years ago. The lower slopes and depression are covered with heather, bilberry, bent and grass on which a few sheep graze. Narrow, sluggish streams flow south-eastwards, through patches of moss and marsh. Grouse are encouraged so that they can be shot, and deer roam here. Occasionally one finds grit scattered on rock surfaces for the grouse. Views from the marked outcrops and boulders take in a great sweep of exciting uninhabited country, miles of it, leading to more hills and mountains. A track leads across the moorland from east to west, but the marked rocks lie to the north of it. One has to work hard to reach them, especially when a gale blows, as it did in November. There are walls, many of them very long, built from stone quarried locally; perhaps some rock-art was removed and is hidden inside them, a practice which is not unique.

There are around 30 marked rocks, so I use the most elaborate to illustrate the motifs. *Craig Hill 1* (opposite) is not obtrusive, and you have to be close before you see it. It is a slightly rounded outcrop, near horizontal, but sloping gently on three sides. It has been scoured by ice, leaving shallow channels that have directed *how* the motifs should be placed, linking cups and cups-and-rings, but there is

Right and below: 9, 10 Craig Hill 1

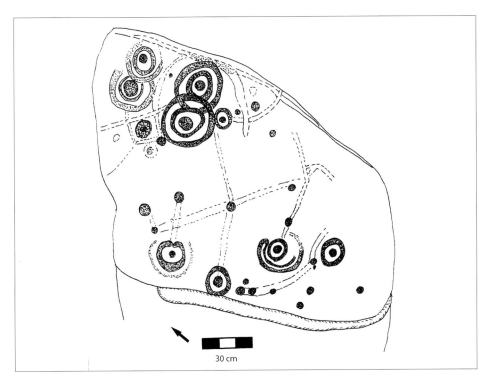

30 cm

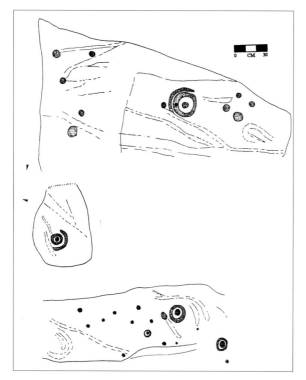

11 Craig Hill 2

a special feature that is very rare in British rock-art: two sets of motifs that are superimposed. There is also a cup-and-ring with a concentric groove that curls back upon itself, again rare, but with parallels locally and in Northumberland and Ireland.

A small cluster of outcrop rocks to the north-east rises from the ground, visible from much further away. There is some quarrying, but cups and single rings remain.

Lower down, and heading for rock-art on higher ground further north-east, is perhaps one of the most exciting discoveries in the area. It lies in what might have been wet ground, a pyramid of outcrop, cracked and split naturally into blocks that have suggested to the motif-makers separate panels for their art (Craig Hill 3). Where cracks intersect, the spaces in between have been used to place motifs, and the cracks themselves are incorporated. Motifs on the lower slopes and at a lower level edge are clearest, as they have apparently been less exposed. The upper slopes of the main panel are covered with faint but profuse concentric rings, and at the edge (north) a small area of rock has been packed with varied motifs (*colour plate 2*).

Other panels formed by the natural structure of the rock have their own markings, including a rare narrow vertical edge with a line of cups. One is always

Above and below: 12, 13 Craig Hill 3

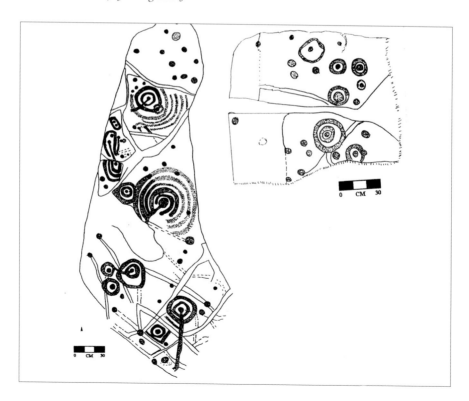

Above and below: 14, 15 Craig Hill 3

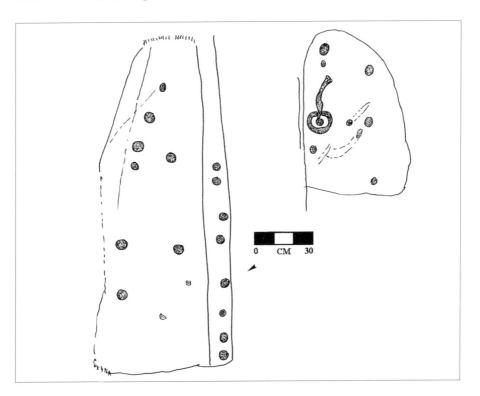

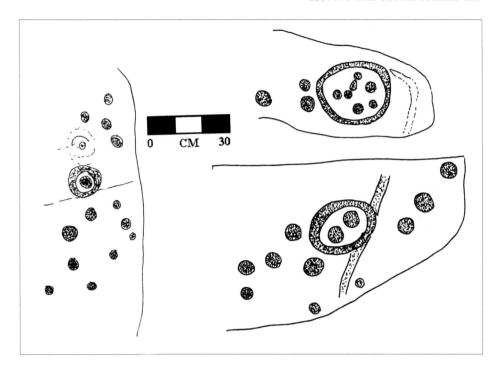

16 Craig Hill 4

ready for yet another variation on a theme. Nearby are other small marked outcrops, not yet drawn.

Higher up the slope to the north-east, divided from the rest by a shallow glacial U-shaped valley which channels water from the hills, is an uneven ridge with decorated outcrop surfaces, one of which is figured here because it is different from all that we have seen so far (Craig Hill 4).

Like all the others, the rock is at a good viewpoint, and mineral flakes in it show white. The rounded south-west end has cups and small basins, and other flat surfaces have cups enclosed in concentric ovals, ending with a scatter of simple cups.

When we look at other discoveries in the area, some made many years ago, we find recorded sites at the Braes of Taymouth and Tombuie to the north-west, then nothing until we reach a site at Urlar to the north-east on a continuation of the ridge. That many of these follow the contour urges us to think of 'trails'.

The wilderness landscape could have been a vast larder for people whose lives were at least partly dependent on hunting, stock rearing and plant harvesting, but there is as yet no sign of any habitations, temporary or permanent. If this was all we had to go on to try to understand why rock-art was there and who put it there we would be stumped for an answer. Although its position in the landscape

Above and opposite page: 17, 18, 19 Croft Moraig stone circle

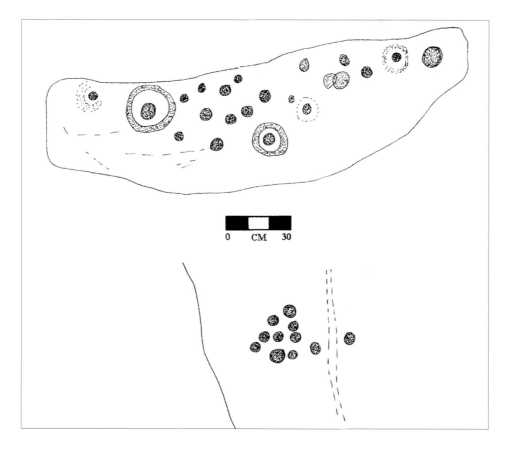

may give us some clue to its function as some sort of signposting, places like these may have been used in other ways unknown to us. We have, however, a repertoire of motifs throughout Britain where there is some kind of association that may offer more clues to time and purpose.

Between Kenmore and Aberfeldy, just off the main road to the south at Croft Moraig is a complex stone circle, built and modified over a long time, as we know from its excavation. The entrance to the monument from the road is inadequate, and needs to be seen to if we believe in good public access, but the site is impressive. There are circles within circles enclosed by a henge ditch and earth and stone wall, with an interior that looks like some sort of maze.

It has recently been established that a timber circle on the site, once thought to pre-date the stones, may date from the Late Bronze Age (Bradley 2005), and that monuments of this late date are linked to the movements of the moon rather than (in the case of Stonehenge and passage-graves for example) to the movements of the sun.

One of the central standing stones has cup-marks, and two of the outer recumbent stones at the edge have cups and cups-and-rings. That they should be incorporated in this monument either could mean that they were marked specifically for it on the spot, or that the marked rocks came in from elsewhere already decorated. Either way, they were important to these people, but we need more information if we are to take this further and this can be done by looking at rock-art in other monuments.

I began this book with observations, accurate recordings, joys of discovery in a fabulous landscape, the involvement of many people's interests and talents, and a mass of questions. Together we will see where other places and stones lead us. Not all rock-art is experienced in a 70mph gale as we had at Craig Hill, neither were all seen in bright sunshine against a cloudless sky reflected in a loch. To miss such experiences, to study rock-art in a building, removes one from a special reality: the power of Place.

What now follows is an overview of the kinds of motifs to be found on rocks, including some representational ones in Europe, a history of the study of rock-art in Britain, where the motifs are found and why, and what conclusions I have reached about their meaning and use. Matters of conservation and display are briefly considered, before considering what effect encounters with rock-art in the open-air has on the young people's art work.

2

Widening our vision: rock-art world-wide

The Eyzies de Tayac region of the Dordogne contrasts strongly with that of Perthshire. It was here in 2005 where I was invited with other world experts to speak about British rock-art and to help formulate a policy for the recording, preservation and display of rock-art that could be recommended by UNESCO to world governments. It is the home of some of the finest cave art in the world, thousands of years older than British rock-art, even older than the recently-discovered Palaeolithic inscribed animals in the caves of Creswell Crags, near Sheffield (a mere 13,000 years old) (Bahn *et al.* 2003).

The conference was a reminder of the unusual nature of rock-art, of its considerable differences in time and place, and of its considerable similarities.

The term 'rock-art' applies to paintings, engravings, picked-out motifs and pictures on outcrop surfaces, monuments and portable rocks. Although it is easy to apply the term 'art' to the dynamic paintings in French and Spanish caves, in the rock-shelters of South Africa or to the continuing tradition of aboriginal painting in Australia, it is not so easy to see a cup-shaped hollow picked-out on a rock surface as 'art', but we use the term as a convenient shorthand. It is the oldest known form of human visual expression.

To try to understand what it means involves us in a detailed study of its environment including all the prehistoric artefacts, dwellings and other 'buildings' in the area.

The art is universal, and although European examples until now have been the best-known and researched, they are only a small part of the world picture. They are easily outnumbered by those, for example, in Australia, Africa and Asia. Robert Bednarik (2004) in *The Future of World Art – a World Review*, published by The National Heritage Board of Sweden, says this of his country, Australia:

> This country, almost the size of Europe, but with a population only a third of that of Italy or Britain, boasts not only the greatest concentration of rock art in the world but also the highest number of rock art researchers relative to population size.

His introduction to his survey carries a very important warning to European interpreters of the meaning of rock-art:

> Australia's rock-art scholars are significantly less inclined to attempt interpretation of rock-art than those of any other world region. It would seem that Australian rock-art researchers are either excessively pessimistic in interpreting rock-art, or other rock-art researchers are excessively optimistic about their powers of interpretative discrimination. (Bednarik 2004)

These are important points that I shall consider in what I say about British rock-art, as I believe that gut reactions or 'vibes' can be quite wrong in trying to interpret what people thousands of years ago meant by these symbols; although people's reactions today may be personally satisfying and exciting, their interpretation has to be based on fact and not supposition. The subjective interpretation of representational and non-representational symbols is fraught with difficulty and danger. Just because we recognise some apparently familiar images such as people, animals, boats and horses, it does not follow that we know what they meant to the people who created the images.

We tend to interpret, naturally, against a cultural and physical background of our own time and place, but can we really reach the minds of people so long ago and see things as they did? In one part of Australia, many different groups of aborigines in the same area may interpret the same pictures painted on rock or drawn in sand in different ways. Naturally, we read into pictures and symbols something of ourselves, as in an ink-blot test.

What do we think of when we see a picture of an elephant: power, destruction, the extinction of wild animals? Maybe, but where the elephant appears in South African rock-painting it may be touching on an important and admirable aspect of its social life, that these powerful giants take collective responsibility for the protection of their young, and this may be the significance of its depiction.

Bronze Age Scandinavian rock-art has many depictions of boats. Do these refer to the seafaring life of the people, the importance of exploration and trade, or are people being ferried from the world of the living to the world of the dead? Symbolism is notoriously difficult to unravel; people often try to make it mean what they want it to mean. We live in an ego-centric universe.

In some ways the problem of interpreting figures that appear to be taken from the natural world has been taken away from British rock-art research, unless the 'non-representational' images are themselves taken from the natural world. 'Abstract' or 'non-representational' images, repeated all over Britain as cups, grooves, rings, triangles, lozenges, serpentine grooves, crossed lines, chevrons,

20 European figurative rock-art
(various locations)

spirals – a whole repertoire that you will find in this book – have given rise to both plausible and bizarre interpretations.

The use of symbols and motifs in Europe reaches a turning point in pre-Roman times; a distinct tradition is halted, but Britain did not even share the later phases of this tradition, its cup-and-ring motifs disappearing in the Early Bronze Age, some 4000 years ago. Thus when we look at British rock-art, we find that after an early flowering, it just stops, and we must ask why. Perhaps there was no need for it; perhaps the values of the societies which produced it became irrelevant as new ways of seeing the world and thinking took over.

Meanwhile on the continent the tradition of depicting scenes from life, such as house-building, farming, fighting, became more important and concentrated, although there was still some emphasis on symbolism in non-representational art.

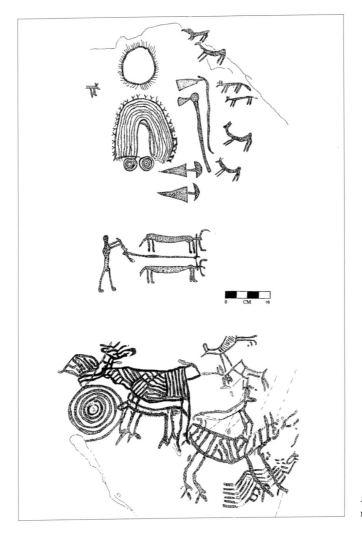

21 European figurative rock-art (various locations)

It is impossible to look at the whole European rock-art tradition here, but some examples are given as pictures, before we look more closely at the British images. I leave the reader to consider what these images might mean.

Should you wish to consider your interpretations against thorough and very well-presented research into Scandinavian rock-art in English, I suggest that you read Professor John Coles' work, *Shadows of a Northern Past* (Oxbow 2005), an example of what rock-art studies should be like.

3

Symbols and motifs

Nothing in British rock-art is painted on surfaces and there is no evidence that colour was added to picked-out motifs. Any colour change would have resulted from the exposure of rock just below the surface, and if this is exposed for long enough, it soon blends in again with the rest, unless it is 'refreshed' with a pick.

Generally the terms *symbol* and *motif* are interchangeable, but I confine *symbol* to a single mark, such as a cup, and *motif* to a combination of two or more symbols, such as a cup-and-ring. Whatever terms are used, they are both a shorthand expression of something that may have had many meanings, perhaps the origins of which were completely forgotten. We do not have to think about how familiar logos came into being: we know what they stand for, and that is enough. I have given examples from across the British Isles; although there are regional differences, especially in clusters of similar motifs, there are more features in common than there are differences. Although there is a distinct preference in passage-grave art for specific recurring motifs, they are also present in landscape-art, in the open-air. Instead of giving a 'vocabulary' of motifs and symbols, as I have done in my other works, I have chosen to arrange the designs on pages that cover many variations, keeping common elements as close together as possible. Inevitably there are many overlaps, as in larger panels a large repertoire of symbols and motifs may be represented on the same rock surface.

THE CUP

The most common symbol, used thousands of times, is the *cup*. It appears on almost every rock panel, either by itself or in combination with others, usually with grooves and with other cups. We have seen it in the Ben Lawers 5 rock, where cups are spread out over the whole surface of a slab, arranged mostly in parallel lines, and differing in diameter.

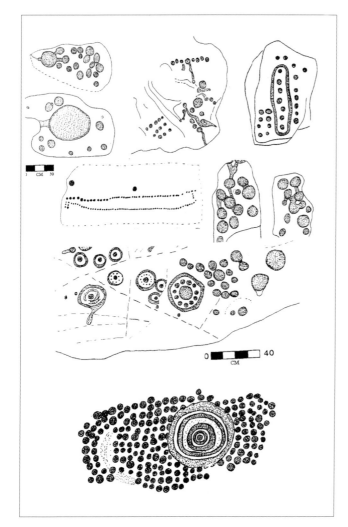

Left: 22 Cups mainly in County Durham, Northumberland, West Yorkshire, The Peak, Kilmartin and Galloway

Opposite: 23 Motifs with linked cups and parallel grooves in County Durham, Cumbria, Kilmartin and Northumberland

The drawings show a variety of arrangements of cups, including the paired 'domino' forms, cups in line, a rare sub-rectangular arrangement, clustered (often referred to as 'pepperpot'), stippled small cups, cups arranged in arcs and circles (rosettes). Generally they are quite shallow, and where they are found freshly made, they are in the form of an inverted cone.

Sometimes a line of cups or a circle may have been intended to be joined to form a line, an arc or ring. Sometimes the cups are so large and deep that they are called 'basins'. Some of these from the inside show that they have been made systematically in sections from the top, with the sides often made vertical. Both cups and basins may be smoothed out either by people or by prolonged exposure, but in most cases the individual pick-marks are visible.

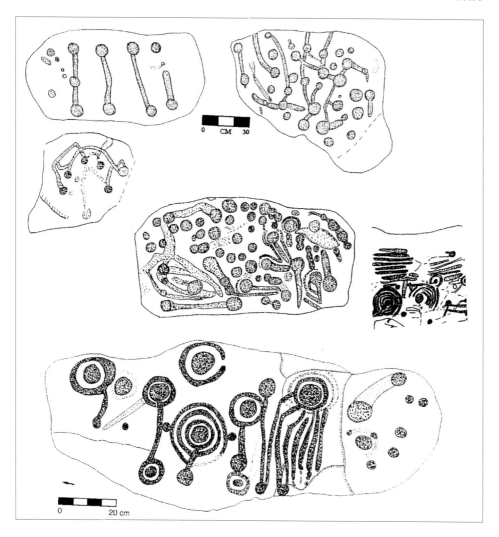

CUPS AND OTHER SYMBOLS

Cups are sometimes linked with a groove (known to some as 'dumbbells'). A large number of cups may be linked with a groove in a line, like a string of beads, following the downward slope of the surface, and these can be echoed by other lines in parallel.

Usually a cup forms an integral part of complex art. The most common use is when it is found at the centre of one or more concentric rings, mostly with a duct running from it. Rarely, one or more cups may be enclosed by ovals, rectangles or heart-shapes. There are some instances where it is clear that cups were already on a rock before being integrated into a later design.

RINGS

The next most common symbol is the ring, either complete or interrupted. The ring may have no central cup, but usually it does. There can be concentric rings up to 12 in number, and these look very impressive. These rings can stop short of the groove that runs out of a central cup (and are called 'penannular', looking like a necklace), or may be cut through by a later groove or grooves. Multiple grooves cutting through rings are rare, but are not limited to one area.

Most rings, although appearing circular, are in fact angular, and it is clear that they were formed by pecking grooves in straight lines from one point to another. Some of them were formed by making a circle of cups, occasionally touching, joined together. This can only be seen on uneroded examples.

Rings can be interconnected, appearing to be packed against one another, but in some cases they are deliberately made to flow into each other, coming close to having a spiral effect. Rings may be closely-packed or widely-spread; in the latter case there may be an inclusion of cups already there or the addition of an arc or circle of cups, though this is rare. Also rare is the superimposition of one set of motifs on another, an example of which we saw in chapter 1 at Craig Hill.

The keyhole pattern is a variation on the concentric ring theme, where two or more grooves run parallel from the rings, leaving a gap to the centre.

When concentric rings are linked by grooves, the effect, especially of a large sloping surface, is one of integration and flow.

Arcs are partial rings, arranged in similar concentric patterns. Sometimes they can focus on a cup, other times not.

GROOVES

Rings are, of course, grooves, but here we look at many other varieties. They are used frequently with cups-and-rings. They can be serpentine, arced, straight, arranged into rectangles, ovals, squares and triangles. They can radiate from the centre of concentric circles, form radiates outside the circle, or be enclosed by a circle. As radials, they can be multiple.

Grooves arranged in a grid pattern are very rare. So too are enclosures formed by grooves ('cartouches') containing parallel lines or other motifs. Zigzag grooves, serpentine grooves and chevrons are more common in specific areas, usually connected with burial, but also occur in the open-air.

In chapter 1 we saw ovoids and half-ovoids. Other enclosing grooves are pear-shaped. A distinctive arrangement of grooves is seen in the making of lozenge

24 A flow of connected cups and multiple rings from Northumberland, Kilmartin, North Yorkshire Moors and Cumbria

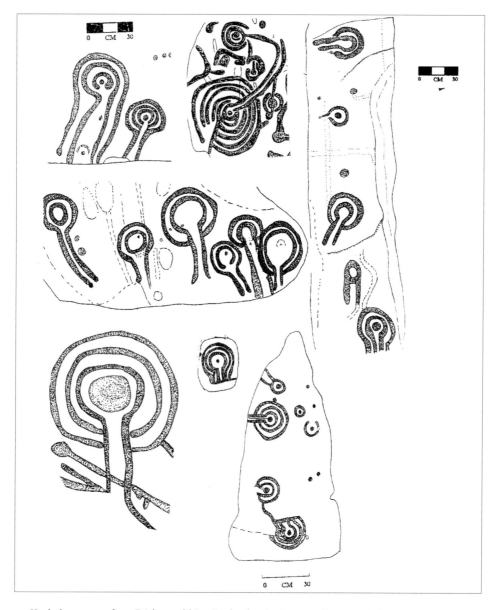

25 Keyhole patterns from Richmondshire, Auchenlaurie, Arran, Galloway and the North Yorkshire Moors

motifs. Grooves form enclosures, and these may be attached to other enclosures, forming distinct designs, and such enclosures may form an annex or appendage to other motifs. A distinct but rare enclosure is the occulus ('eye-shaped'), where two cup-and-ring figures join. The term spills over to the 'spectacle' motif, where the rings are further apart and joined by a groove.

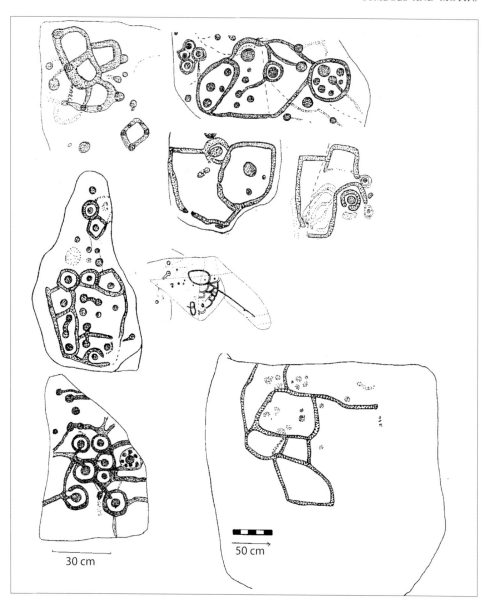

30 cm

50 cm

26 Grooves as enclosures, from Dousgill (D), Gayles Moor (D), North-West Yorkshire, Northumberland, Kilmartin and the North Yorks Moors

One function of the grooves, either straight or curved, is to divide a rock surface into zones. This is combined with an awareness that the natural cracks and grooves already on the surface can be incorporated in this zoning and paralleled by it.

SPIRALS

Spirals vary from those that are merely an unfurling groove from the end of a stem, like a shepherd's crook or frond, to complex combinations, right-handed and left-handed, that sometimes run into others. Some are horned, some are combined in threes, some are single grooves and others double. They may stand by themselves or are combined with other motifs. Some do not appear to have been successful, and are hybrids. The different types are best seen in the drawings

It is possible to produce all these designs with a hard stone tool, as people have demonstrated, particularly the recent efforts of Martin Murphy at Kilmartin, where he has made a replica of part of the Ormaig stone with a basalt pick mounted in a

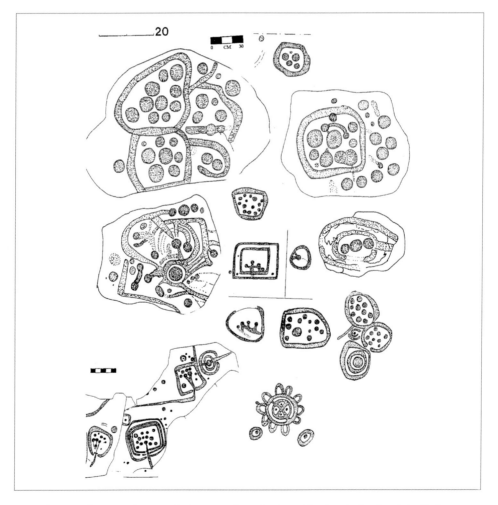

27 Enclosures of various shapes enclosing cups, from Durham, Northumberland and the Peak

28 Some motifs isolated from panels by Avril Purcell at Iveragh; lower: a selection of van Hoek's motifs from Donegal

wooden handle. He and Dr Anne-Sophie Hygen (Directorate for Cultural Heritage, Norway) have discussed with me the intriguing question: if the making of these motifs was so important, what happened to the fragments and dust produced by the picking? Was the dust just allowed to fall to the ground or was it collected? Martin's theory is that it could have been incorporated into pottery material.

Martin, who created the superbly-crafted wooden round table in the Marion Campbell library and other furniture at Kilmartin, has used basalt as the choice of material for his designs on metamorphic rocks, producing the kind of excavation marks that we see in pristine rock-art. This kind of work is essential to our understanding of prehistoric methods of marking rocks, which includes the use of hand-held tools (Beckensall 2005, p.15).

29 Spirals and other enclosed motifs from Newgrange (top 3), Morwick (3), Long Meg (C) and Orkney

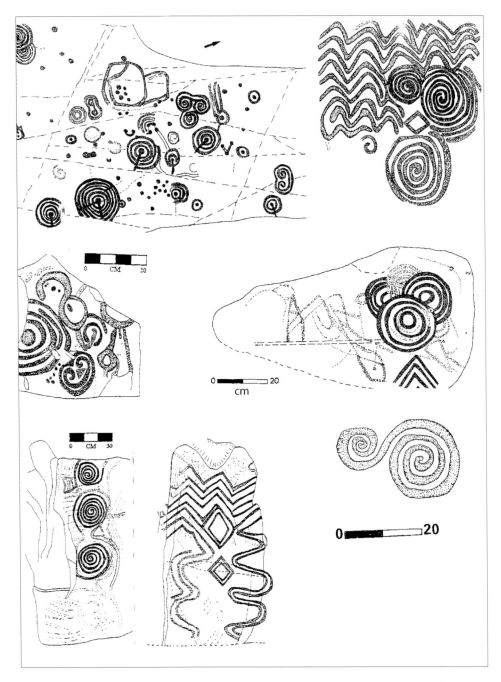

30 Spirals and related motifs: serpentine grooves, chevrons, and lozenges – from Achnabreck, Newgrange, Lilburn (N), Glassonby (C), Anglesey (2) and Gallows Outon (G)

31 Complex spirals and other motifs from Morwick (N), spirals and serpentine grooves from Clear Island (Kerry) and passage-grave lozenges and cross-hatching in Ireland

4

How the study of British rock-art began and developed

Ireland, home of some of the world's greatest rock-art, had some early references to its passage-grave art, one as early as 1699, when a Welsh antiquarian, Edward Lhwyd, described how workmen had carried off some of the stones from the Newgrange mound, marked with crude and barbarous sculpture that he thought must have been pre-Roman.

Lhwyd made careful notes on all that he found there, and left some very good plans of the discovery, including sketches of the decorated surfaces inside the corridor and chambers. There were many visits after this by travellers and antiquarians, who based much of what they wrote on Lhwyd, and the kind of information they handed down has been of value to those who have excavated the passage-graves recently.

Camden's *Britannia* has a cup-and-ring stone drawing thought to be on a Druidical altar, and in a later edition, 1806, he described Newgrange as 'a pyramid formed of pebble or coggle stones' covering slabs of cists with spirals and a trellis-work of small-lozenge forms, all, of course, put there for Druidical rites. In the *Handbook of Irish Antiquities* (1848), William Wakeman illustrated and described a 'great variety of carving, supposed by some to be symbolical'.

In England, discoveries were made later on.

J.C. Langlands discovered some worn and defaced figures incised on a rude sandstone block, near to the great camp on Old Bewick Hill in north Northumberland. Though strange and old-world looking, these figures then presented an isolated fact, and he hesitated to connect them with by-past ages; for they might have been the recent work of an ingenious shepherd, while resting on a hill; but on finding, some years afterwards, another incised stone of a similar character on the same hill, he then formed the opinion, that these sculptures were very ancient. To him belongs the honour of the first discovery of these archaic sculptures....

32 Tate: Old Bewick

It was George Tate, the Alnwick historian, who first explained how the discovery of the first rock-art in the 1820s began in Northumberland. No one could have been more outside what we think of as mainstream archaeology than John Charles Langlands, whose family was famous for making fine silverware in Newcastle. What made him give up the idea of being in the family business and moving to Old Bewick, a small village north of Alnwick with his wife and children, must have been the lure of farming. At this he excelled to such an extent that he was commended in official reports for the way in which he treated his workers, for they tended to stay with him when others moved periodically during the 'hirings', and he trained and kept his farm managers. He also was one of the first farmers to realise that better conditions of housing helped keep itinerant workers.

Langland's interests were many. His daughters helped at the local school, and one of his greatest contributions to the community was his part in the restoration of Old Bewick church of The Holy Trinity, one of the loveliest in the county. Born on 27 March, 1800, John became tenant of Old Bewick in May 1823, and died in 1874. He is commemorated by a cross at the end of the Kirk Burn Lane, on the road to Chillingham, and his sons and wife have plaques in the church. The sons were army officers, one killed in New Zealand and the other in France. The daughters are not commemorated in the church, but we can read about them in the school log books.

33 Old Bewick landscape, including the excavated cairns at Blawearie

John Langlands was in many ways typical of the kind of curious observer who would have been aware of the landscape around him and what it contained. Old Bewick village lies at the foot of a Fell Sandstone scarp, the kind of formation that has an abundance of prehistoric rock-art sites, burials, and enclosures. At Old Bewick there are two particularly interesting pre-Roman enclosures joined together like a pair of spectacles, poised at the edge of the scarp above the valley of the River Breamish, which here changes its name to the Till.

There are smaller enclosures on the scarp edge, a disturbed burial cairn which has a cup-marked cobble dislodged from it, and a large, quarried cairn in a dominant position. The site brings together many prehistoric monuments, but it is particularly important for its rock-art.

The large block of glacially-moved sandstone, with a gently-sloping surface, was chosen for the addition of cup-and-ring marks linked by grooves flowing down its surface, interconnected and interweaving, and by a row of horizontal cups and others on three vertical surfaces. We now notice that someone had begun to dig in grooves for wedges to split the rock, but had abandoned the idea. We also notice that the surface was weathered in such a way that it already suggested circular designs, and that these irregularities were exploited on the top with cups and cups-and-rings, and with the enhancement of a large, deep oval basin (*colour plate 23*).

34 Old Bewick rock in 2006, with a row of cups on the vertical faces (scale: 50cm)

There is another large block of stone close by, decorated less profusely, and in the field sloping down from the hillfort are many cup-and-ring marks, with variations on the theme. Some are embedded in the enclosure's outer wall; others have survived recent field clearance of heather and stone for pasture. Langlands knew nothing of this profusion, but he would have known the importance of much of this marginal land as an extensive burial-ground, for there is an abundance of cairns. Many show the tell-tale signs of having been dug for treasure: a hole on top, and collections of worked flints, pottery, shale and jet objects, for shepherds with time and acute observation would have sought out possible sources of riches, only to be disappointed, for there was nothing of monetary value – just curiosities. Some cairns, we now know, have rock-art incorporated in them.

In the 1860s interest in the area was directed at the large burial mounds such as that at Blawearie, when the ubiquitous Canon Greenwell paid it a fleeting visit with workmen armed with picks and shovels. He found graves in it, pottery and a jet and shale necklace, but left a considerable amount for me to excavate in more scientific times. Overlooking the site, further along the scarp is Hepburn Moor, aptly named, as it means high ground with burials, some of which are still visible.

Prior to that, Greenwell had found a site at Roughting Linn, in 1852, which George Tate visited with him, pulled 'nine inches depth' of turf off it, and exposed several sharp and distinct motifs. Later that year Greenwell read a paper on them at the Archaeological Institute in Newcastle and, 'though two ponderous volumes professing to be a record of its proceedings have been printed, strange it is, that this paper, the most novel communication made to the meeting, found no place in this publication'. It seems then, that rock-art was not everyone's flavour of the month!

Dr Johnson, secretary to the Berwickshire Naturalists' Club, published the Roughting Linn stone in his *Natural History of the Eastern borders*, so at least someone was taking an interest.

Tate reckoned that these Northumberland discoveries stimulated interest in other parts of the country through the Society of Antiquaries of Scotland and in the *Metropolitan Journal*. However, he pointed out that the real work of discovery had been in Northumberland, where 'several members of this club and their friends have been quietly, yet successfully, exploring the district'. It became so detailed that Tate was asked to get everything together and publish it. He took longer than he expected, because it was difficult to get accurate drawings and because he had hoped that some excavation would have thrown more light on what they meant. He did, however, manage to draw all those known, all but Roughting Linn on the same scale, with the help of an artist, John Storey, based on rubbings and tracings.

He acknowledged help from, among others, John Langlands, adding:

Here, therefore, the geologist, the antiquary, and the artist have united to produce, as far as possible, correct representations of these time-worn sculptures.

Tate is a man after the field-worker's heart. He says:

Oftentimes, as I have experienced, days may be spent in wild exposed moors and hills, with no gain save negative results.

He puts his cards on the table with his presentation:

I wish it to be distinctly understood, that in this paper I shall deal more with facts than fancies; and as I shall give an account, not only of the inscribed stones themselves, but also of the ancient remains with which they are associated I believe, that a collection of authenticated observations will have their value, even though we may not arrive at a full and satisfactory explanation of the symbolical figures; for such an extensive survey of the subject will of itself dissipate some of the crude notions which have been formed as to the meanings of the figures, and which have been founded on a limited knowledge of the facts bearing on the question.

His survey covered 53 sculptured stones in Northumberland with 350 figures.

When in 1853 George Tate had read a paper to the Berwick Naturalists' Club. Mr J. Collingwood Bruce was impressed with Mr Tate's 'sagacity' and agreed

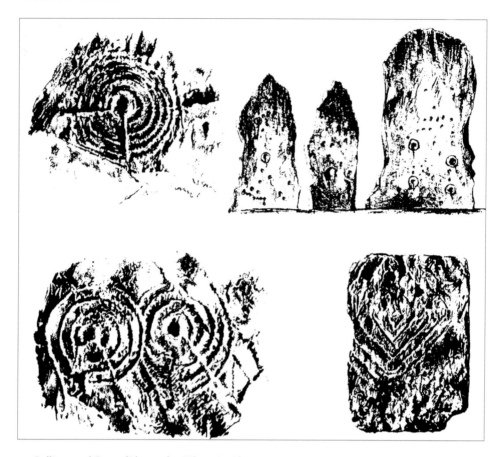

35 Collingwood Bruce lithographs, Kilmartin Glen

that the carvings had 'a common origin, and indicate a symbolic meaning, representing some popular thought'. The Rev Greenwell in 1863 took up the theme again, this time with the Tyneside Naturalists' Club, and told them that: 'They differ from all other symbolised expressions with which we are acquainted, and seem peculiar to the Celtic tribes which once peopled all Western Europe.'

His work on British barrows was well-known among the learned, and urged others to investigate further, although his methods did provoke some contemporary criticism. Interest spread; local history societies were inspired to explore and record, they attracted speakers of note, and this interest included rock-art. Leisure, money and a good formal education ensured that their findings were presented to others. High-quality lithographs, photographs and drawings were part of this recording.

When Tate read a great landmark paper in 1864 to the Berwick Naturalists' Club at Bamburgh, the President remarked that the subject was 'in its infancy' and:

what we want, and what we have to wait long for, a key, which, like the famous Rosetta stone, will enable us to read and interpret these remarkable inscriptions, engraven so long ago upon the Northumbrian rocks. Whatever may be their import, now so mysterious, they cannot fail to prove, when their meaning is discovered, of very high interest.

Mr Collingwood Bruce, who produced splendid lithographs with the help of the Duke of Northumberland, gathered together current research to make his own position clear.

He felt that one tribe had made the marks, and that if one discovered many more in Europe it would be possible to trace the movements of these people. He found evidence of the *period* of the rock-art in areas 'abounding in remains of the kind usually styled Ancient British – camps, burials and (rarely) standing stones.'

Bruce found that there was no satisfactory answer to the *intention* behind them. He rejected the idea that they were maps of camps, warned readers of the Druidical sacrifice theory, and was not convinced that they were 'sun symbols'. He said that 'it is highly probable that these incised markings are, in some way or other, connected with the burial of the dead', and was supported in this belief by Canon Greenwell.

If we connect the circular marked stones with interments, we advance a considerable way towards an explanation of their meaning; for this implies that they have a religious significancy.

In the Duke of Northumberland's collection of local material at Alnwick Castle are drawings by Mossman that are similar to those produced by Tate.

Tate drew other parallels from Malta, Penrith, Pickering, Dorchester, Ireland and Derbyshire. When he asked what they might mean, he swept aside the argument that they might be plans of camps, preferring to see them as a symbol representing some popular thought, telling of 'the faith and hope of the original inhabitants of Britain'. He added: 'Beyond these general views, I confess we wander into the regions of fancy and conjecture.' After some speculations, he says:

Those who are not content unless every mystery is fully explained may feel dissatisfied, that after all the labour research bestowed on the inscribed rocks, we cannot read them off as from a lettered book. ... Something, however, has been achieved – materials for aiding in the fuller solution of the problem have been placed on record – an advanced starting point made for future enquiries – and a

36 A selection of Sir James Simpson's illustrations of (top to bottom): Rothiemay circle, Bamfshire; Moonbutts, Perthshire; Lancress Cromlech, Gurnsey; Clynnog-Fawr cromlech, Wales

description and representation preserved of marvellous sculptures which time and the elements will eventually obliterate.

That sums up the stage that all of us reach in our researches.

The other significant writer and researcher in this field was Sir James Young Simpson, Bart., M.D., DCL, Vice President of the Society of Antiquaries of Scotland, and of the Cambrian Archaeological Association, one of Her Majesty's physicians for Scotland, and Professor of Medicine and Midwifery in the University of Edinburgh. That is how he is described as author of *Archaic Sculpturings of Cups, Circles, &c. upon Stones and Rocks in Scotland, England and other Countries.* It was published in Edinburgh by the Society of Antiquaries in 1867, thus providing another landmark work along with Tate's. As we see, he is a man eminent in disciplines other than archaeology, who became fascinated by rock-art. Like others at the time, he also quotes Sir Thomas Browne's dictum:

Time, which antiquates antiquities, and hath an art to make dust of all things, hath yet spared these minor monuments.

The book was to provide a learned and solid basis for anyone wishing to know more about cup-and-ring marks. A scientist, he made careful, factual records of all that he encountered, and did not speculate unless there was good reason to.

Scottish antiquarians were already taking a serious interest. As long ago as 1785 an 'incised slab' that covered a cist full of cremated bones at Coilsfield in Ayrshire had been drawn. In 1830 Archibald Currie published the first brief regional survey of rock-art, the cups-and-rings of Cairnbaan in *Description of the Antiquities, Etc., of North Knapdale.*

Sir James analysed motifs – how they were made, what they looked like, of what common elements they were made up, and in what contexts they were found, going beyond the bounds of Scotland to do this. One has an insight not only into the man himself, but into the contacts that linked the learned and comfortably-off who had the time and inclination to research, including many clergymen in rural parishes. He always acknowledged debts to his scattered friends and acquaintances. He received information from them, and incorporated it into his book in his style. He omitted no detail, including precise measurements. He ensured that his illustrations would not only be informative, but attractive, through 'the artistic skill with which Mr Richie has produced the Lithographic Plates'.

He brought his vast scientific experience and the worlds that it opened up to him to his hobby. It provided a way of seeing and communicating his discoveries by crossing subject boundaries. His approach was to study the main elements in cup-and-ring art, to show some deviations from these, and to describe how they were produced.

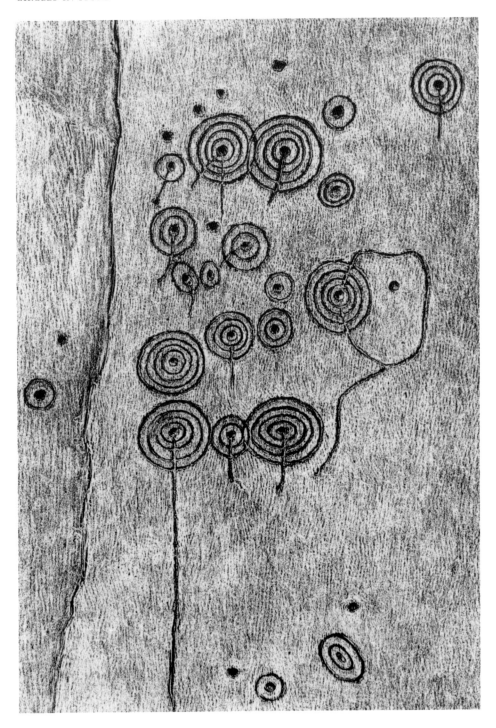

37 Cairnbaan; Sir James Simpson's 'Carnban'

The second section dealt with the locations of rock-art, beginning with those in monuments, for some of the earliest discoveries were made in the previous century, and needed to be included in his corpus. We see them in stone circles (without the popular tendency to attribute them to Druids), in avenues of stone, cromlechs, tumuli, cists and urn covers, and on standing stones.

It is interesting that he should take these locations first, as some tend to go for the wider spread of rock-art within the landscape, but he saw that attributing a function to them could only be explained in this way. Some that he recorded have now gone, but we have his words and pictures. Like us, he was fully aware of how much of our past has been lost through land clearance and ploughing.

He did not confine himself to Scotland, but pursued similarities elsewhere, incorporating Northumberland, Welsh and Yorkshire monuments as he went along. He pursued the context through 'underground houses', fortified buildings, ancient enclosures and camps. He left the connection of motifs to the dead to follow those connected with people's lives, in round houses and in or near 'ancient towns (oppida) and camps'. He moved into Northumberland territory for further examples, drawing on information from 'my friend, Mr Tate, of Alnwick' and the Rev William Greenwell. He reiterated what he had already seen in Tate's account and praised 'an elaborate series of large and magnificent drawings made by Dr Collingwood Bruce'. He drew attention to the proximity of rock-art to settlement sites, such as Beanley, Old Bewick and Dod Law, and reminded us that the links persisted in Yorkshire, Wales and Cornwall. Throughout, he drew on information sent to him by people he called his friends. It is clear that there was a brotherhood (no sisters mentioned) among the early antiquarians.

Art in the landscape was another category for exploration, especially those examples with no connection to settlement – the only visible evidence that there had been anyone there. He noted that 1852 was the first publication of Northumberland sites, then said (without point-scoring) that Scotland had produced an account 22 years earlier by Mr Archibald Currie, who was formerly 'a schoolmaster at Rothesay' (what would we have done without these inspired amateurs?), who described the Antiquities of North Knapdale, Argyll.

In an interesting aside, Sir James directed us to theories that may be both ridiculous and serious. The innkeeper at 'Carnban', known as 'The doctor', interpreted one rock-art panel as echoing 'astronomical plates for elucidating the revolution of the planets around the sun'. He avoided comment simply by quoting his informant, then got on with the more scientific task of recording what was actually to be found on the stone, in a good drawing.

The largest panel of rock-art in Britain, at Achnabreck ('Auchnabreach') naturally took up space in illustration and description. He also referred to the possible meaning of the place-name, something that always interests me

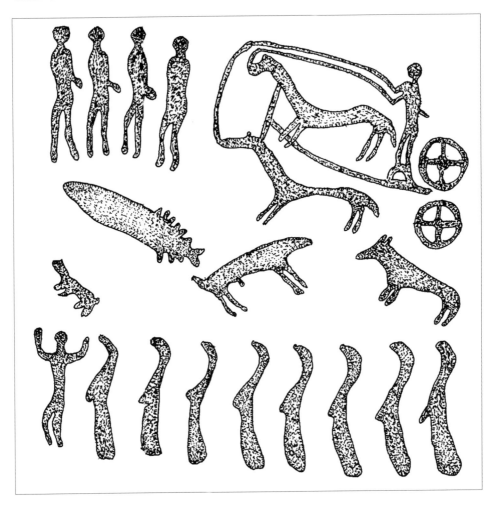

38 Kivik: part of a slab-setting in a massive mound in Sweden (SB)

in the sites that I record. The final part of his study of Scottish stones was of portables.

The emphasis then moved to other countries, beginning with 'Lapidary sculpturings in Ireland'. He was fascinated by the imagery of the chambered tombs, but uneasy about chronology. He visited Newgrange with 'my friend, Sir William Wilde', on whose illustrations he drew for his own. He thought that the elaborate motifs and their skilled execution placed them later than others that he had dealt with in Scotland and England.

His 'lapidary' trail led him to Brittany, to tumuli and cromlechs, which he thought ought to be considered 'a still more advanced type of art than that of Ireland'. The current thinking appeared to be that the more skilful the art, the more sophisticated and later it was. Again, he drew on the help of many friends to help him record all this. When he reached Scandinavia, he wrote:

I am not aware that the active school of Archaeology in Scandinavia has hitherto paid any special attention to archaic pre-lettered carvings upon stones and rocks.

However, he found many interesting examples in the cromlechs of Denmark; he wrote of boats, crossed circles, cups and human figures, and illustrated the spectacular interior of the Kivik mound in southern Sweden from the work of Professor Nilsson, who saw it as a commemoration of some victory, probably naval, 'by worshippers of the eastern sun-god Baal' in the Bronze Age. He added, after lengthy discussion, 'Perhaps, however, in the presentation of his ingenious and elaborate interpretation of the Kivik carvings, Professor Nilsson has wandered too far from home,' as they were more probably native, not foreign, in a very wide-ranging dissertation on this fascinating site.

His chapter ended:

I am assured by my friend Professor George Stephens of Copenhagen, that examples of stones in Scandinavia, with cup-and-ring cuttings, are by no means so rare as the silence in regard to them of Northern Archaeologists would seem to indicate.

He realised that the search in Britain was in its infancy, and this applied also to the continent of Europe; discoveries all over Europe would

bring to light new facts, both as to the sculptures and themselves, and as to the ethnological relations which may possibly prove among different portions and locations of the human race.

The book seems to have grown as he went along, for the last section covers some of the same ground, showing a reinforcement or modification of his ideas. He began with high-flown language beloved of that period and of some of today's writers:

They are archaeological enigmatica which we have no present power of solving; lapidary hieroglyphs and symbols, the key to whose mysterious import has been lost, and probably never to be regained.

I will not take you along the path of tracing some proposed hypotheses on how the motifs began and what they might mean, but he had another go at Professor

Nilsson's belief in their alleged Phoenician origin, drawing on a vast bibliography to reject the theory. This occupied a whole chapter, with more footnotes than text.

The link with 'religious' monuments was well attested, but he argued that it was impossible to date them accurately because there was insufficient data. He used the rest of his book ('at the risk of some repetition') on their pre-literary appearance, their connection with 'dwellings and sepultures', the character of finds associated with them, and their geographical distribution.

He was doing what many of us have done since: gathering evidence objectively as a basis for understanding, and not looking for facts to fit theories. In his thinking Sir James was careful to point out that the discovery of motifs on a portable stone established the *latest* date for its use, but that the carving could be earlier. He also saw that 'the reverence for the sculptures themselves had died out in the minds of the generations who used them as simple building material'. He noted that the freshness or erosion of the carvings must be carefully considered too. As more carvings were left on 'the tombs of the dead than on the dwellings of the living', he saw this as the best way to provide a period for their manufacture, as it was possible that accompanying artefacts could be dated. He warned that the period of use of any ritual monument could be extensive, though, with barrows being used for secondary interments. Pottery sealed in by a cist gave a final date for the use of the motifs. He thought that there was still enough data to show 'the kinds of implements which co-existed and were buried with those men whose sepulchres show the ring and cup carvings'. There was more information in Brittany where 'much more successful enquiries have been made than in our own country'. He was clearly well-informed there, and on work in the Channel Islands, where the 'silting up of cavities' had produced a chronology all of which was characterised by stone implements.

He was convinced that the beginning of cup-and-ring art must be in the Stone Age, and that the practice continued through to the Bronze Age, although at that time no bronze objects had been found in burials connected with cup-and-ring marks.

He noted that it was 'very rare that we ever find early pottery display any of the circular or spiral lines, and then only when it approaches, or comes within, the Bronze Age'. Combinations of circles, spirals and zigzags were the geometric patterns seen on 'the most ancient bronze ornaments and weapons'. He concluded that cup-and-ring marks were earlier than representations of natural or artificial objects.

If such symbols could be of a metal age, were they formed with metal tools? Areas like Northumberland had soft sandstone, but elsewhere surfaces were hard. This did not mean that metal tools had to be used, however. He used a 'flint celt and wooden mallet' on schist. In Edinburgh Museum the doorkeeper used a 3in-long flint, 1in wide and ¼in thick with a mallet to cut 2/3 of a circle into granite in 2 hours. It was 7in in diameter, cut ¼in deep and ¾in wide. He noted that the sharp tips of the flint broke off from time to time, but by turning the flint round, another sharp edge was formed. He had solved his problem by experiment.

In the British distribution of rock-art he found 'they all evidently indicate wherever found, a common thought of some common origin, belonging to a common people'. But what race or races made them? He delved into literary sources for what was known about early Britain, but field monuments pointed to a much earlier race. There was enough data to equate them with the building of megalithic monuments, cromlechs and stone circles in Britain, the Channel Isles and Brittany.

> It appears to me not improbable, therefore, that the race of Megalithic Builders, whether Celtic or Pre-Celtic, who had tools of flint and polished stone, first sculptured our rocks and stones with the rude and archaic ring and cup cuttings. But the adoption – and even more extended use – of these forms of ornamental and possibly religious symbols passed down, in all likelihood (with their sepulchral practices, and with other pieces of art and superstition), to the inhabitants of the Bronze Age, with its era of cremation and urn-burial, – and thence onwards to other and later times; and perhaps they can be still traced in the spirals, circular and concentric figurings upon our ancient Celtic bronze weapons and ornaments; on their stone balls and hatchets; on ancient bone implements and combs.

> It is important, at the same time, to recollect that the *origin* in cup and ring cuttings may still be older than even the age of the earliest Celts or of the Megalithic builders.

Sir James Simpson's contribution to the study of rock-art, with its repetition and emphasis of certainties and problems, is enormous. Everyone who wrote about rock-art referred to him and to others like Tate, but mostly in fragmentary reports of random areas, made piecemeal.

In the 1880s Romilly Allen compiled a list of cup-marks in Scotland. In his general observations he found them free from design in the arrangement of cups and thought that they might have been executed 'one by one, at different times, either by the same or different individuals'. He saw cups-and-rings as 'a well recognised symbol frequently repeated', connected with burial rites. At Ilkley, in his third paper in 1882, he dismissed suggestions that they were star maps, doodles, picture writing, or games. Because they were executed by more than one individual at different times, and by their proximity to tracks across high

39 Simpson's Loughcrew

ground they may have marked routes to sacred high places, like Baildon Hill. He favoured a Bronze Age date for them, rather than their being a continuation of an early Neolithic tradition.

In West Yorkshire, now with about 670 recorded marked rocks, an early report in 1869 by C. Forrest and W. Grainge was entitled *A Ramble on Rumbold's Moor, among the Rocks, Idols and Altars of the Ancient Druids in the spring of 1869*. This title suggests that they could not have read very deeply, but it included illustrations of carvings. In the same year 'ancient markings' were published in the area of the Cow and Calf rocks on Ilkley Moor. When in 1879 Romilly Allen wrote the two papers (mentioned above) for *The Journal of the British Archaeological Association* on *The Prehistoric Rock Sculptures of Ilkley*, more serious interest began to be shown.

A publication called *Baildon and the Baildons* by W. Paley Baildon, F.S.A. came into my hands recently. It was privately printed for the author and sold to subscribers only – at 6s per part, at the beginning of the twentieth century.

Baildon mentions several people who had recorded marked stones, and he visited some of the carvings at 'Dobridding' with the Assistant Architect of the Corporation of Sheffield, Joseph Rycroft, whose drawings are reproduced in the book, and one photograph by W.E. Preston. Mr Rycroft drew clearly, without any shading, and to scale. This brief acquaintance plunged the author into some speculation:

> my knowledge of them is almost entirely derived from the works of others, and I have not made a special study of prehistoric antiquities.

The others were Tate, Simpson and Allen, which he dipped into before laying out his own theory. He thought that any theory had to take into account the widespread distribution of carvings in many parts of the world, and the constant repetition of marks. His conclusion was that they were depictions of 'ghost houses', based on the idea that spirits linger after death and that they required attention from the living – including a house to live in. The house could be real, a miniature copy, or any other representation, such as cup-and-ring marks, which were used long after their original meaning had been forgotten, and were mere ornamentation. A cup could have been one house, and the rings the stockades. He thinks that such a theory would satisfy the Tates, Simpsons and Allens. So,

> The large rock surfaces covered with carvings, such as Roughtin Linn, I attribute to ghost villages, where a new ghost-hut is made at each death.

He reckons that the unique ladder motif at Ilkley 'could be made by a tribe who cultivated the hill sides in terraces'.

I mention this one theory of many because it illustrates the frustration of people not knowing the answers. Whereas some offer theories with diffidence, others have assurance sitting on them like 'the hat on a Bradford millionaire'. Ever since these markings were discovered there must have been hundreds of explanations, sadly without factual support. The number of papers multiplied, but there was little interest among professional archaeologists. Then it lay fairly dormant.

The interest in rock-art research left Britain for a while, apart from chance finds, and blossomed in Europe. There an interest grew in the way the art was distributed, its age, and typology. The Abbe Henri Breuil gave an important Presidential address to the Prehistoric Society of East Anglia in 1934, and in 1957 O.G.S. Crawford published *The Eye Goddess*. At this time an emphasis was placed on seeing rock-art as some sort of representation of humans. Breuil in his lecture looked at the relationship between tombs and open-air art, and did not see them as different. He collaborated with Professor R.A.S. Macalister in Ireland, among others.

The 1970s in Britain brought Ronald Morris' work to the fore, and that of the present author. Ronald was a solicitor with a passionate interest in rock-art; he had sufficient means to travel widely and to meet many people on the continent who were engaged in the study. He published extensively; much of his work does not have the benefit of modern technology, especially the use of computers, but this is no criticism, for his fieldwork was extensive and thorough. He also aimed at writing books for everyone, and many have derived their interests from his regional Scottish studies, where he was the first to open up areas such as Argyll and Galloway to the general public. He published extensive data covering Britain. He was fully aware of the dangers of unprovable theory about the meaning of rock-art, and is famous for his collection of suggestions gleaned from literature and hearsay about them.

No one could have gone forward very quickly without his groundwork, and he followed the best traditions of the Scottish antiquarians not only in his methods but in his personal integrity and consideration for others.

He donated his archive posthumously to me because I was someone he thought would continue the work and because he liked what I wrote. It was impossible for me to deal with that and my own work, so I donated it appropriately to The Royal Commission on the Ancient and Historical Monuments of Scotland. I still use his camera, which always reminds me that his presence is still with us out in the field.

Evan Haddingham produced his accessible study of rock-art in 1974, *Ancient Carvings in Britain: A Mystery*. What the public wanted at that time was not a learned tome, but a book that showed through its illustrations what rock-art is

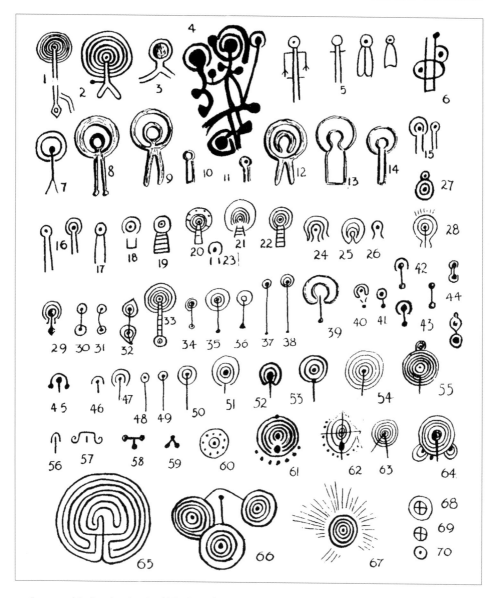

40 In 1934 this drawing by the Abbe Breuil sees rock-art as depictions of humans

about, and to express the author's enthusiasm in reasonably simple language. This was a good start.

In 1980 a book by Jean McMann on 'Rock Carvings of Ancient Europe' called *Riddles of the Stone Age* was a collection of very good black and white photographs of sites across Europe covering rock-art in passage-graves, the landscape, and Maltese temples, interspersed with text reflecting on what they might mean.

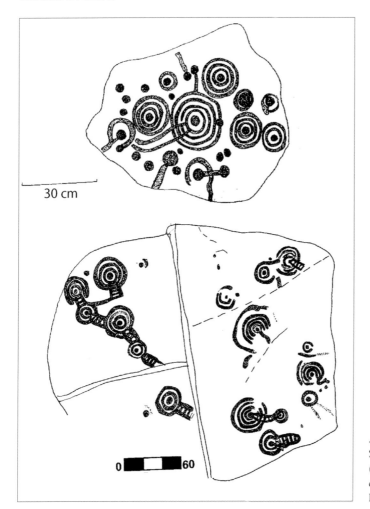

30 cm

0 ◼◻◼ 60

41 Ladder motifs:
Standing Stone Rigg
(NYM) motifs seem to
develop into ladders at
Ilkley

Because there was little interest shown by professional archaeologists, and because most publications at that time were southern-England oriented, research tended to be confined to articles rather than books, and those of us who were determined to present our research both more fully and in a readable form chose the difficult path of publishing it ourselves.

Maarten van Hoek, living in Holland, has contributed much to the recording of sites here, beginning with two slim publications on north Northumberland, and extending his range throughout the British Isles with the speed of someone who has another life and a teaching job. Not only did he re-record known sites, but discovered and recorded new ones. Since then he has extended his range world-wide, through his own web site and a stream of articles in international magazines and journals.

Many researchers have been influenced by what was happening in Europe, and many visited the Valcamonica sites in northern Italy, where rock-art study seemed to take on the aura of a mystic crusade. Many have also turned to Scandinavia for inspiration.

Today there is a great deal of cooperation among the major agencies of rock-art research and many personal contacts which enrich everyone.

A brief excursion into rock-art by Colin Burgess looked intelligently at the issue of chronology. Perhaps the most important development for rock-art studies was the arrival on the scene of Professor Richard Bradley, one of the brightest and most approachable of modern archaeologists, and research by a new generation began to place rock-art as a vital part of our development, and not as a fringe activity left to enthusiastic independents. Elizabeth Shee in Cork added great expertise in her wide-ranging investigations of megalithic art from Spain to Orkney. Recent work by Ian and Irene Hewitt (now at Bournemouth), Paul Frodsham (Northumberland National Parks Archaeologist) and Tim Laurie brought interesting new thinking to the study. The work of those mentioned here, and others, is listed in the Bibliography. What is very gratifying is that we now have so many enthusiasts who discover new marked rocks and report them to us. There has been a considerable amount of new data published, not only in books, but also in papers. Apart from the well-known journals, the new *Northern Archaeology* (The Bulletin of the Northumberland Archaeology Group) under the editorship of Paul Frodsham, became for a while one of the most influential in producing new research quickly and to a high standard.

Ireland, of course, has its great professional tradition of research, especially in passage-grave art, but hitherto unknown rock-art in the landscape has also appeared. It was astonishing to me to be invited to open the new lecture hall at Castlebar, County Mayo, to give a talk on British rock-art and to present rubbings that I had made of the Bohea stone for hanging in large glass panels on the new library walls (*colour plate 24*).

A second panel had been found in the west, recorded admirably, and may be yet another stepping stone to the discovery of more (see chapter 5).

I cannot mention all those working in this field, but I do want to draw attention to continued voluntary (i.e. unpaid) contributions. At a time when there is real conflict in England between independents and professional involvement in archaeology, I have not personally found the relationship at all uneasy. A major book which appeared in 2005 on *The Prehistoric Rock Art of the North Yorkshire Moors* is the result of years of work by Graeme Chappell, Paul and Barbara Brown, who are brilliant fieldworkers with other jobs. They have found hundreds of rock-art panels and by sheer persistence have pursued references and found lost ones. One area of their discoveries was on Flylingdales Moor, where a large fire later burnt many hectares of heather and exposed much of what they had already found, and more. At a meeting of the English Heritage Advisory group I had established that it was important for such discoveries to remain the literary property of the finders until they were published, and this, after some awkwardness, may now be followed as a principle. My own role is to encourage the greatest cooperation between professional and voluntary archaeologists, especially now that so many people are moving into the rock-art domain.

There is always a danger of people trying to grab media attention to enhance their own reputations as a result of a superficial brush with rock-art, often by producing some unsubstantiated theory that the public may like. This happened when the Fylingdales Moor cairn kerb was presented as the world's oldest rock map, with mountains, dwellings and birds! This is very tiresome and unprofessional to those of us who have spent years carefully considering evidence that is acquired with much time, effort and great patience.

Links between rock-art researchers have always been strong. A strong link between groups for a while was Stuart Feather, based largely in West Yorkshire, but researching with his group into County Durham and the North Yorkshire Moors. He followed a tradition established by Arthur Raistrick and Eric Cowling, who in turn provided the impetus for the work of a voluntary group based on Ilkley, whose major publication is *Prehistoric Rock Art of the West Riding*. This was through the efforts of Anne Haigh, Sidney Jackson, Bill Godfrey and through the two authors of the work, Dr Keith Boughey and Edward Vickerman – both teachers.

There have been other surveys of areas, but the major surveys, except for Cumbria (by the author), have been mentioned above. There is no doubt that there is much more to come. English Heritage's survey, after a lapse in which little happened, has been followed by the funding of a project for Northumberland and Durham County Councils to record all their rock-art under Dr Tertia Barnett. Clearly, most of this has already been done, but hopefully more aspects of it, helped by the training of a new team of volunteers, will come to light.

Among the professional archaeologists who believe not only in devoting considerable time to field surveys but also to excavation, there are several in the new generation who, like Dr Clive Waddington, are probing deeply into real issues rather than giving all their time to 'management' issues. His kind of work is well supported by other professionals like Dr Aron Mazel, who has brought his great experience of African rock-art and museum work to the north of England. Christopher Chippindale and George Nash have also brought new insights into rock-art from an international point of view.

Interest has blossomed on a worldwide scale, and in Britain it is interesting to see universities setting up specialised departments of rock-art, and offering post-graduate qualifications in its study. We must not forget our roots, though.

My own interest in British rock-art owes much to the early scholars. By a fortunate coincidence, unknown to me at the time, the very rock that triggered Langlands' interest triggered mine. It was not exactly a road to Damascus, but that huge block of marked rock was a turning point. I was soon to learn that we didn't know much about rock-art, and I set out like these early antiquarians to find out, not as my main occupation, but as a hobby, as a small part of my life. In retirement I have had more leisure to pursue this hobby more thoroughly.

A lack of interest in rock-art among professional archaeologists has probably been due to the fact that the study of rock-art was not the best career move. It involves considerable exploration of the landscape on foot, with not a great deal to show for it, apart from an increase in fitness. Even when sites have been found and recorded the bewildering questions about how the marks originated, what they mean and why they are where they are, are so open-ended and in some cases unanswerable that many have ignored them. Even now, despite the increase in interest worldwide and the amount of research being done, many find it difficult to incorporate rock-art into a thesis on the Neolithic. There are other interesting and safer areas of research that produce more impressive results more quickly. Only recently has this changed. When the great panel of rock-art at Chapel Stile in Cumbria was discovered, some people who visited it thought that it must have been done very recently because no one had found it before. It takes experience to assess what are natural marks, what are artificial and how artificial marks were made.

5

Art in the landscape

Most marked rocks in Britain are to be found in the landscape, numbered in their hundreds, thinly spread, but occurring in clusters. The major concentrations are in northern Britain and in Ireland there are distinct clusters in the north-west (Donegal) and the south-west (Kerry and Cork).

There are statistical methods that can be applied to their recording and study. All such sites can be plotted accurately with the aid of a GPS. What can be seen from them, and from how far, can be recorded. The rock types, such as igneous, sedimentary or metamorphic, and their hardness, are also noted.

Although some rock surfaces appear to us to be more 'suitable' for marking, cracked and undulating surfaces within the same area are preferred, so we have to try to understand why. One reason is that an irregular surface and other irregularities may already have some of the elements of design that people were looking for. Could some other, incomprehensible, element have determined the choice of rock, such as it being at a special place, perhaps where something important had happened?

We must look for signs that markings were made at different times on the same rock surface, for superimpositions, for indications that designs could have been re-cut. Symbols/motifs must be classified, and the interrelationships of these motifs examined to find out, if possible, in what order the motifs were entered. With a range from simple to complex (which may be our aesthetic judgement), we may look for a pattern in which more complex motifs appear in different areas or at different heights, so that we may decide whether some combinations of symbols appear in special contexts.

All these observations must take into account the relationship between where the rock-art appears and other archaeology, such as: settlements, including fields and domestic sites, scatters of flint, chert and agate left by temporary settlers, defensive enclosures, artefact finds, monuments, burials and routeways.

We must take into account how much of a rock surface has actually been marked. This may depend on what was covered by vegetation in prehistoric times; in some cases the decoration was framed by leaving a space around it at the edge of the rock. A good example of this is at Ballygowan (K). In other cases, such as Achnabreck east (K), only the upper part of the surface is marked, so the lower might have been covered with growth.

We must distinguish between what appears to be a random scatter of symbols from a deliberate design. The problem here is that a single cup-mark could have been as significant in its context as a deliberate design. The modern viewer may be more impressed by size and variety. Some archaeologists have distinguished cups and cups with single rings as 'simple' motifs, and others with multiple rings as 'complex', yet a pattern of cup-marks arranged in lines, rosettes or dominoes can be equally 'complex'. However, as a general rule the addition of many rings does seem to us to produce a more arresting display than a single ring, without our knowing what the addition of extra rings actually meant. Some have considered the possibility of rings being added over a period of time, but there is no evidence for this.

There is a similarity throughout Britain in design elements. Thus rings without a central cup are rarer than rings and a groove centred on a cup. The sameness is broken when some individual seems to break away from the norm and produces something novel like a rosette, or enjoys joining together cups of different sizes with a groove, as at Kilmichael Glassary (K). The spiral breaks away from the usual. Squares and other angular enclosures are rare.

The most striking differences appear when we consider relationships between the design elements on a rock. These always take into account the natural form of the rock in its slope, surface smoothness or otherwise, the presence of natural cracks or glacial grooves. Natural and artificial are brought together. Direction of slope determines how much sun the rock surface receives at different times of the year, and shadows play an important part in revealing what has been pecked onto the rock. We look at the pattern from the lower slope upwards, but can stand above the design and look around to see what areas of landscape are encompassed from there. What appear to us to be the most sophisticated designs (and therefore the most satisfying aesthetically) are interrelated motifs. Some run into each other or touch. Ducts running from cups may run parallel. Motifs are enclosed singly or in groups by cracks. It is this grouping of symbols and motifs that produces 'complex' art.

What follows is an insight into some of the areas where landscape rock-art occurs, to see what common features they share, or otherwise. I begin in Scotland.

The Scottish Royal Commission surveyed rock-art of the Strath Tay *area* in 2000 and identified 121 marked rocks where previously there had been only 14. I am grateful to Alex Hale (Hale 2003) for his published account of these decorated rocks, as I was able to record only a small number of them. The loch

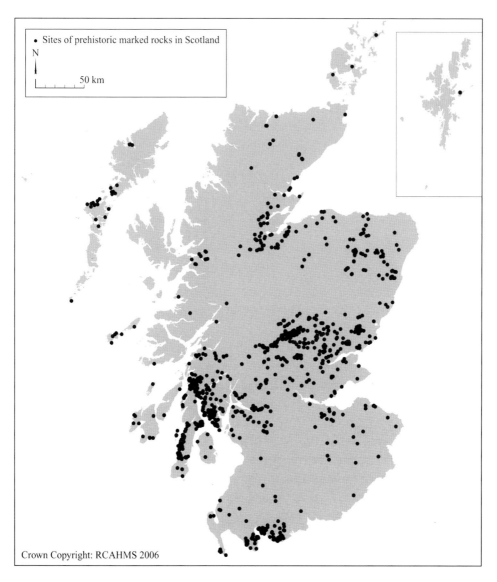

Sites of prehistoric marked rocks in Scotland

N

50 km

Crown Copyright: RCAHMS 2006

42 Map of Scotland's sites. *Crown Copyright: RCAHMS*

is long, with steep slopes on either side that are mainly tree-covered. The north slope (south-facing) has a foreshore up to 200m OD, and a 1km-long terrace between 200-400m high made up of well-drained soils and glacial drift, littered with boulders and with some bedrock outcrops. This terrace is relatively flat to the south and gets steeper to the north (Beckensall 2005, map on pp.129).

Above 400m the land is bare of trees, with open moorland and three big peat basins. Today it is used for grazing, and in the recent past was used for 'shielings'

– temporary herds' huts and gardens when beasts were being pastured in the summer. The lower and middle slopes are used most today.

The 14 sites previously recorded included 21 cup-and-ring-marked rocks, two of which could not be relocated. The newly discovered sites are in four concentrations, with a dispersed group to the west, a tight group of eight rocks further east, 70 dispersed boulders or decorated bedrocks, and 12 rocks at the eastern end. The gaps between the clusters of marked rocks pose a question: were there any there originally? Have they been removed by farming? Does the dense vegetation of the loch shore cover some? How many have found their way into walls?

Alex Hale reported that at least 10 per cent of known marked rocks have been removed: four appear in buildings, three in enclosure banks of dykes (walls), five in clearance heaps and one in a rockery.

His analysis shows that of the 121 marked rocks 16 are on bedrock outcrop (three have cups-and-rings, the rest plain cups), with four on the lowest and 12 on the middle bands. 105 are on boulders, all in the upper band, with only one cup and single ring rock in the lowest band.

All the views from the rocks are naturally to the south and south-east, but in the past the views may have been obscured by vegetation; that has to be determined by examining ancient soils. On the highest ground there is a concentration of marked rocks at springs and stream sources; lower down the ground has been cleared for pasture. The marked rocks do not dominate the landscape, and can only be seen from close by. More prominent rocks have no markings on them, so the emphasis is on marking rocks that already blend in with the landscape – a blending in rather than dominance.

The more elaborate designs show evidence of sequence, additions and alterations that could have been made at any time. Some of these are illustrated in chapter 1.

The distribution shows most below the head dykes on cultivated land, but the most dramatic designs are on the higher ground. What does this mean? Bearing in mind that finds are made by chance often by individuals, a regulated search like this that has revealed so many new marked rocks makes an assessment more confident. It has been noted, for example, that the marked rocks are related to the boundaries of different soil types – a point that is seldom noted. In the past, as now, vegetation would follow that distribution. In Alex Hales' words: 'they are related to the character of the ground, probably as indicated by the particular type of vegetation'.

Increase in data allows us to reassess previous research, such as that of Margaret Stewart (1959) and Richard Bradley (1993). One conclusion is that the more elaborate rock-art in this survey does appear at a higher level than simple cups, but that the latter continue to take their place alongside the former and that the lower ground is not devoid of cups-and-rings. Another observation is that when we talk about 'complex' motifs, we must remember that one of the panels illustrated here shows how elaborate a pattern can be by using only cups.

One particular observation that my friends and I made in Strath Tay that tied in with what we had discovered previously, particularly in County Durham, was the coincidence of some marked rocks with stream sources, where 'viewpoints' in Durham were limited. The other major point is that rock-art here blends in with the landscape and tends to avoid the more prominent rocks.

As many of Britain's regions have been subject to quite intensive recording, the reader is directed to these reports. Some regions are surprisingly lacking in rock-art, even when there is an otherwise strong prehistoric presence, particularly the south of England. Regions like Northumberland and West Yorkshire have had a long tradition of research, but even so there has been a surge in the number of marked outcrop and earthfast rocks recorded. Others have surprisingly few, like Wales. The Peak District has few, but there have been some notable new discoveries. Galloway needs a fresh and thorough survey, with potential for more sites to be discovered among those many open-air sites of which we know. County Durham and adjacent areas have many more sites recorded recently, with important concentrations being uncovered. Cumbria used to have most of its rock-art in or on monuments, but new discoveries are now changing the balance.

How new sites are discovered is of great interest. One may anticipate where they might be, following up clues already given. Much depends on individual interest and enthusiasm. Some teams have been formed to re-examine known sites, and inevitably more will be found as a result of this.

It is not in everyone's interest, though, to have new sites discovered. Recent examples of this come from Cumbria. At Copt Howe/Chapel Stile, where Paul and Barbara Brown discovered the now famous stone block on the route to the Pike o' Stickle and its Neolithic axe quarries, there was a distinct opposition to the site being scheduled, as it was used by rock-climbers for 'bouldering'. This means that people were climbing all over prehistoric art. I find it difficult to believe that, despite surveys and the number of people walking in the area, that no one had seen the rock-art before.

Were people deliberately keeping quiet about it? When the markings were examined by father and son, both professors, in a recent paper that asked the question of whether all the markings were Neolithic or much later, I had a long meeting with them at which it emerged that the site had been known for years, as a seasonal resident 60 years ago was known to one of the authors as a man who went around making marks on the rocks. It is possible that he added

43 Copt Howe/Chapel Stile, Cumbria

to the ancient markings already there in an act that we would now regard as vandalism, for rock-art had been widely recognised in the north and publicised since the 1840s. There is no problem with the 'cups' on the vertical face, as these are natural, although as we know from other sites, natural features that already act as cups could be incorporated into a design. Did this man really lie on his stomach to execute patterns? I would suggest that any additions to the rock-art would probably have been made by his standing up. The rock is very hard, and would require great skill and patience, especially the multiple, closely-packed concentric circles that we see there. Perhaps one day the area beneath rock face will be excavated to see if the motifs reach further under it, and if there are chippings of stone or even the evidence of a tool. The implication that some marks may be natural is beyond dispute, as those of us who have spent years among the motifs are fully aware of distinguishing twisted bedding planes from artificial markings. Fortunately the rock is scheduled, and has become an official responsibility that no one will be allowed to damage it in any way. The whole surface has now been laser-scanned, which helps to verify the original survey of what is on the rock. R.N and R. S. Haszeldine, who wrote their searching article about the rock (Haszeldine and Haszeldine, TCWAAC Vol. III, 2003) wished to add:

Thus the carved face deserves protection against human contact, to preserve it and adjacent soil profiles for scientific investigation (a note to the author which did not appear in the article).

Another recent discovery of predominantly cup-marked outcrop south of Ullswater (Beckensall 2002) with outliers that included ring marks has also drawn attention to further possible discoveries, including a site at High and Low Park, Crummock Water discovered by Dr Tim and Eileen Sowton, where a prominent partially-quarried rock is covered with cup-marks. I recorded these and handed further investigation over to Durham University researchers. The importance of sites like these cannot be overrated, as they all show that Cumbria shared the same urge to decorate outcrop rock as their contemporaries did in Northumberland and Durham. They also targeted prominent places in the landscape, the sides of valleys that are so crucial to communication in the mountains. Of particular importance is the route that led from the Neolithic axe-manufacturing regions along the valley to Lake Windermere, as the export of these highly-polished axes was highly desirable to people all over Britain, emphasising the importance of trading and cultural contacts as long ago as 5000 years. We now move across the water to Ireland to consider another important aspect.

It is important to think in terms not just of excavating monuments, but of as much of the landscape around them as possible. This improves our understanding of why the rock-art is in the landscape, as Blaze O'Connor has demonstrated with a recent excavation in County Monaghan (O'Connor 2003). At Drumirril her excavation was designed to find out what happened around rock-art, supported by geophysical survey which revealed, for example, prehistoric pits close to marked outcrop. On another site the marked outcrop was enclosed by a banked enclosure with a re-cut external ditch, stone revetment and possible post-holes dating to numerous periods in prehistory, the earliest being the Neolithic. It means that around these sites marked with motifs there was a great deal of activity involving 'investment of considerable time and energy' and that the places where rock-art is situated are very significant at many periods of prehistory. This is worth stating again here, for although I am looking specifically for the significance of rock-art in burials and other monuments, rock-art of any kind has a much more widespread significance, and that we must see everything – burials, stone circles and decorated outcrop and earthfasts – as all part of the same tradition and meaning over hundreds of years.

In Ireland the Loughcrew Landscape Project (*Past*, the Newsletter of the Prehistoric Society, No.51, 2005) is designed to do just this. There are clusters

44 Loughcrew cairn and panorama

of cairns on the Slieve na Calligha Hill, Carnbane West and the Patrickstown summit, a particularly well-known cairn being 'Cairn T'.

The sites look over the central Irish landscape from a dramatic position. Investigation has now switched to the land below Slieve na Calligha, with the identification by Elizabeth Twohig of a stone circle, henge, standing stones, open-air rock-art and cist burials which show that the use of this lower landscape was as important as that of the tombs themselves. The project, designed to study this area, has already located a new cup-and-ring rock-art site:

> probably the most extensive example of cup and ring decoration known so far in Ireland outside of County Kerry, with over 65 separate elements identified.

Isolated rocks with motifs may have a particular importance to later generations. At *Bohea*, an outcrop is covered with cup-and-ring marks, with the addition of Christian crosses, as it lies on a pilgrimage route to the important mountain of Croagh Patrick. I recorded this with rubbings when I stayed at the house next to it. In the grounds of the house was a piece of tragic Irish history, a small burial ground of unmarked stones where victims of the Famine were buried.

45 Bohea, or St Patrick's Chair: a rubbing

I gave the rubbings to the owners of the house, and these records have since been mounted in glass panels and adorn the walls of the Castlebar library. Since my visit, other outcrop panels have been discovered by a geologist, Colm Jordan, at Drumcoggy Mountain, with a full report now published by Christiaan Corlett (Corlett 1999). The site (NGR 10752/27122) is not easy to find and reach, as there are old peat workings to cross; the marked rocks are on unusually high ground at 350m (compared with Iveragh at *c*.175m) on hillslopes that form a hollow overlooking an area of wetland from which peat has been taken. Not visible from the site, but close by, is Loughanshee, a small permanent stretch of water. Much of the land is today covered with blanket bog, but so was the Kilmartin Glen, Argyll, burying a prehistoric landscape that included cairns, stone circles and decorated standing stones. Found in 1995, the rock-art is on the lowest slope of an exposed sandstone, varying from coarse to ice-smoothed, with cracks and natural small indentations that seem to have directed what kind of motifs were to be made and where they were to be placed (as in so many other parts of the British Isles). There are similar exposed areas suitable for marking. The motifs are simple:

46 Drumcoggy Mountain. *G. Bracken*

circular, about 10cm in diameter, the circles being very precise. In addition to complete circles are arcs, penannulars and cups, the latter on their own or forming the centre of rings and arcs. Altogether, 130 motifs have been recorded. Some of the larger cups form shallow basins, an idea which may have come from natural indentations there. They form a distinct regional set of motifs, and are in an area not only devoid of other rock-art, but of any other prehistoric remains.

For this reason, it is not easy to decide why they are there, but their position in the landscape may be concerned with mobile groups using the area in summer to water herded animals or to hunt at water holes. This was certainly my impression when I visited it. The site does not give the widest view of the landscape, but narrows it to the low-lying wetland. It is difficult to know whether it is on a 'trail' on a natural pass across the mountain summit. There may be other reasons; we do not know whether agriculture was possible, and as the name of the nearby lake translates as 'lake of the fairies' this may not be of any literary significance if you are looking for 4000-year-old 'spiritual' or 'ritual' places.

Croagh Patrick, on a pilgrimage trail from the Bohea stone and other sites, but not from this one, exhibits a phenomenon know by its recorder, Gerry Bracken, as the 'rolling sun' for at specific times of the year the sun sets by 'rolling' down one side of the triangular mountain. The mountain is still a centre of pilgrimage, visible for miles around.

Although great attention has been paid to passage-graves in the bend of the Boyne because of their remarkable rock-art, nowhere near enough attention has been given to accurately recording rock-art in the landscape. Although the list of sites has at least doubled since 1946, information about the rock-art is not very accessible. The general public and others do not always find journals the best way of learning about rock-art. Therefore, comprehensive coverage is much needed.

There has been a great surge of interest, though. Dingle and Iveragh, Donegal, County Cork, County Louth and County Carlow have produced many pieces of rock-art, and smaller concentrations come from County Meath, west Wicklow and Kilkenny.

A measure of how much there is in the landscape is indicated by Maarten van Hoek's work in County Donegal (van Hoek 1987, 1988). Beginning with established, recorded sites, his intense and rapid coverage of these areas has not only added to the recorded motifs on the rocks, but also has resulted in the discovery of many new sites. One of the main areas there is Doagh Isle, now a peninsula, which, like many Irish sites, is coastal or close to the sea. The art there occurs on outcrop surfaces that are smooth and flat, where the largest number and most complex of motifs concentrate. It also occurs on outcrop ridges with a more restricted range of motifs, and on irregular outcrops projecting above the ground, mostly boulders, with only cup-marks. It seems then, that where there is a choice, what we consider to be the best surfaces are used for the finest designs. In some areas where there are, for example, only earthfast boulders are available (as in County Durham), they will be used to their fullest limits for decoration.

Van Hoek's visits have added so many discoveries to his data that eventually he was able to record 160 cup-and-ring marks, 164 parallel grooves, four sets of oval rings and three keyholes. Care must be taken with statistics as, if we are numbering sites, we have to define what we mean by that. Usually a site has to be some distance away from another, and all the rocks within that site with decoration then belong to it. Counting motifs does not get us very far, as the importance of motifs is how far they are spread over one rock, what kinds they are, whether there are any superimpositions, and how they compare with others either in the same area or over Britain as a whole. What has emerged from van Hoek's work is a pointer to the potential of going out into the field and finding more, then recording them to the highest possible standard. This takes a great deal of time, skill and organisation, and money, especially if you are working independently.

47 Magheranaul drawing. *Based on M. van Hoek*

Some of the most outstanding rock-art panels have been found by van Hoek, particularly at Magheranaul, where the repertoire of motifs includes a cup with two rosettes and a ring, a 'cartouche' design containing 10 parallel pecked grooves divided in two by another groove, five large shallow 'disc cups', one of which has four concentric rings. Other rocks in the same area have an emphasis on parallel grooves, one elaborate series with a cup-and-ring at the centre. These rocks lie on the slopes of a low hill occupied by fields, heather, grassland and gorse. The views from the rocks, to the south, are across the tidal bay to the mainland, and the quality of carving makes this place a very significant one.

On other sites there is a high incidence of concentric rings around a cup, with no groove leading out, particularly at Mervagh, where the rock-art lies isolated in an area where it is otherwise sparse. It lies on a rough slope only 200m from the Mulroy Bay, which penetrates deep inland. Its position is prominent, with wide views over the bay and the hills beyond. Van Hoek notes that although the ridge has many suitable places for art, the extreme northern part was chosen, where it is fractured and ends in a steep cliff. The ridge and the steep eastern slope are covered with motifs (van Hoek 1988). Here we have the dominant cup and concentric ring motifs and the fascinating variation of a cup with two concentric rings surrounded by a rosette of eight or nine small single-ringed cups.

In 1986 a field study was undertaken in Ireland to bring recording up to date so that rock-art could be better understood and contribute to Irish prehistory. Susan Johnston reported this in 1991 (Johnston 1991) as part of an Oxbow monograph on 'Rock Art and Prehistory'. She refers to 116 rock-art panels, of which 51 are in Kerry and Cork, as well as giving attention to those outside these areas.

By 'sites' the survey meant those rocks which had more motifs than just cups, found to be on outcrops and earthfasts, with a very few on standing stones. All were pecked, none showing any signs of added colour. The motifs are cups, rings, rectilinear-shapes and some unclassified types. Some had grooves, mostly from the central cup. The 65 study 'sites' had 1938 motifs, of which 1074 (55 per cent) were cups, 694 (36 per cent) circular, 136 (7 per cent) rectilinear, and 34 (2 percent) of other types. Because they share similar symbols, the motifs were thought to be contemporary in date.

In the landscape the survey found that motifs were in areas of arable land, but on outcrops and boulders which would have been a hindrance to farming. They are all on hill slopes, often overlooking fertile valleys and arable flat lands – more accessible than the rock-art which overlooks them. They are close to water sources. The relationship between rock-art sites and settlement was not tested. They are more scattered but less numerous than the four types of megalithic tomb, close to settlement areas, and part of everyday life. Only two of the 48 sites still in situ were considered difficult to reach. Some motifs show signs of being applied at different times and some were re-pecked. The author sees them as being revisited over a long period of time, being added to and refurbished.

One of the most interesting regional surveys was undertaken by Avril Purcell on the Iveragh Peninsula, and was included in *European landscapes of Rock-art* (Nash and Chippindale 2002). In her early research days she was closely associated with the Reading University surveys in Galloway, Kilmartin and Northumberland conducted by Richard Bradley, from which we all learnt a method of examining art in the landscape.

The area is dominated by an east-north-east–west-south-west oriented mountain range with deep U-shaped valleys, lakes and rivers. It has the largest concentration of rock-art in Ireland. As in other parts of the British Isles, the motifs are abstract and geometric, ranging from simple to complex compositions, mostly concentrated in specific locations rather than scattered over the whole area. There are over 120 sites, many close together at the heads of river valleys, and these were the main subjects of the survey. She abstracted 24 motifs, with the usual variety shown in British rock-art (see chapter 3). All were considered to be of roughly the same period, and all were on sandstone.

Her method of study included how much could be seen from the rocks, places from where the rocks could be seen, their accessibility in this rugged landscape, the relationship of hill slopes to passes, a comparison with what can be seen from unmarked stones, and the proximity to water.

She discovered that some were in accessible areas along routeways and rivers, but others were in difficult and dangerous places overlooking these accesses. Types of motifs and sizes were examined in context to see if there was any 'controlling logic' in where they were placed. These proved to be consistent with the results of other studies in Northern Britain.

Her conclusions were that there was a difference in placement of motifs between those located at viewing points and those located along routeways. Uncarved rocks had wider views. Those at viewing points were the most difficult to find, so people had to know where to find them, and what hazards they faced to reach them. There is a suggestion that some people were not given access to some of them.

Some locations have a high proportion of carved rocks in a cluster, with exclusive motifs, suggesting a particularly important place. Close to rivers, themselves providing routeways, is a common location chosen for carvings and these are easy to find as other routeway carvings are.

The actual choice of motifs does not depend on where they are placed, either at viewing points or on routeways. Simple and complex exist together, although a group is sometimes dominated by one type. In isolated areas the art tends to be more elaborate. There are local variations within the five clusters in the study area. Some overlook water, but this is natural in a culture of pastoral nomadism, especially if the climate was warmer.

To return to Scotland for a moment to draw a parallel, a large outcrop at Loch Michean, Kilmartin (Beckensall 2005), covered with large, small and simple-ringed cups lies at a stream source, from which the water flows to Loch Michean

48 Loch Michean (K).
Paul Brown

500m to the south. The choice of the rock for carving is obvious, for had the motif-makers wished to do so they could have chosen another surface not far away that would have commanded a view of the whole of the west coast. Instead, the markings are sited in a funnelled direction towards the loch, and the route either continues from there to the Kilmartin plain or southwards through the hills to Ardifuir, at the sea.

Avril warns us not to apply generally the results of the study of one concentrated area to others. There are trends, but local knowledge was fundamental to the distribution of carvings. The difficulty or otherwise of reaching a marked rock in a vast landscape is more important than the composition of the carving. It would be interesting to see what kind of finds there might be around some of the rocks to give us more information of the people who made the motifs (see chapter 3 for the main motifs).

Open-air sites are seldom excavated, and when they are, excavation may not lead to exciting results; what we consider 'negative evidence'. In the Peak District of Derbyshire (Barnatt and Robinson 2003), there is a rock outcrop at Gardom's Edge, Baslow where the rock-art became so endangered by exposure and by someone actually using bleach to 'clean' the rock in 1994-5, that it was decided to make a fibre-glass replica and cover the original with it. Excavations around the rock at the same time showed no associated structures or ritual pits, and only a small number of chert and flint flakes.

This brief survey of open-air rock-art across Britain enables us to dwell on some general characteristics. Very few decorated rock surfaces are vertical, and these have produced some remarkable results. Outstanding is the cliff face rising out of the River Coquet at Morwick (N) with its varieties of spiral motifs. Its position on a major river with access to sea and hinterland, wide and deep enough to be navigable by small boats and a source of food, close to a fording place may account for its importance, justifying the effort of those who would have found it difficult to peck motifs skilfully so high up on the cliff face. That the predominant motifs should be spirals, with a rich variation on the theme, without any context other than their position, and equal in design to those in passage-graves, on the east side of Britain, makes it unwise to label them as 'passage-grave art'. Similarly there is a site at Hawthornden near Edinburgh where a cliff recess also bears spirals. The site lies 8m above the River North Esk in a deep gorge, with two vertical surfaces decorated, one with a double spiral, an S-shaped spiral and others. The left face has six or seven 'triangles', six circles, three concentric rings, and something described by Morris as 'scutiform' (like a shield) (Morris 1981).

The most interesting recent discovery was made in Ayrshire on a red cliff overlooking a tributary of the river Ayr, in 1986, recorded by Jack Stevenson. There is a predominance of cups-and-rings, three animals, radiates from a cup inside a central ring, and other motifs that are not easy to identify. Modern technology has been brought in to record this, a laser scan by the Royal Commission, which demonstrates the effectiveness of this technique. Many superimpositions have been located (*colour plate 6*).

49 Ballochmyle setting. *Crown Copyright: RCAHMS*

50 How Gill (D), at a stream source

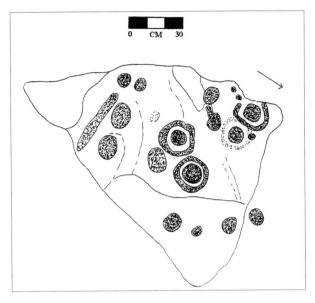

51 East Loups (D), a cupped triangular slab at a stream source

We have already seen that the block of volcanic tuff at Chapel Stile is decorated profusely on its east face, this being the best surface. At Old Bewick (N) the block of sandstone that is covered with cup-and-ring motifs on its top surface also has single lines of cups placed horizontally on its vertical surface.

Mention has already been made of the way in which stream sources and other water sources such as ponds and lakes are decorated. Some are hidden. At Cotherstone Moor, at E. Loups rock 6 (D), close to a possible early enclosure that pre-dates the abandoned farmstead, a boulder is almost buried in a narrow stream bed near its spring source. Roughly triangular in shape, the boulder has 18 cups, some of which are large, three with single rings.

At Howgill, overlooking the Hury reservoir in Baldersdale (D) is a flat, wet, field with a profusely-decorated slab of Millstone Grit embedded horizontally in an area from which springs rise, below a ridge on which there are several cairns and a burnt mound. Whether the 'stream image' of a long groove running through a cup-and-ring from a cup, covering almost all the length of the rock, is influenced by the idea of a stream, is conjectural (Beckensall and Laurie 1998).

52 Barningham Moor, Eel Hill

The streams that rise on Barningham Moor (ibid.), flowing north and dropping steeply to the valley below, have many panels of art, some of them situated on natural mounds (some with added cairns) that are like stepping stones through marsh. Further south, Osmonds Gill cuts the scarp as a strange, deep, dry valley that has no surface water except for the powerful spring that rises at the lower entrance to the gill. Although there is no stream, the sound of water can be heard underground after heavy rain. Rocks with markings more elaborate than simple cups favour the vicinity of springs and streams rising from Osmonds Gill and the northern slopes of Eel Hill.

On Gales Moor (ibid.) there is a particularly interesting rock (no. 3), in Folly Enclosure, covered with cups linked by grooves, lying in a small valley between two linear, glacial, low hills just above the place where the spring emerges. Again, could the grooves echo the water flow?

At Cairnbaan a profusely decorated flat outcrop slab is often in soggy ground. There are many other examples and it is to be expected that springs and streams flow from the places in the landscape where rock-art is at a view point, for water makes its way to the valleys below.

High Banks, Galloway, has rock outcrop with a massive coverage of high-quality designs, based largely on cups, and one reason for their being here is that it is a dried-up small lake or pond. Water, as a source of communication, for trade, as a route to penetrate the hinterland, or an essential for watering animals, was crucial. Coldmartin Loughs, Northumberland (Beckensall 2002), is of interest in this respect, for an area of high undulating-sandstone and thin soils has loughs that would have been important to pastoralism. Looking down on the loughs are some panels of rock-art, the slope on which they are situated directed towards the water.

Right: 53 Folly
Enclosure: at a
stream source on
Gayle's Moor (D)

Below:
54 Coldmartin (N):
loughs surrounded
by marked rocks
(*far right*), with the
Milfield Plain to
the left of the scarp

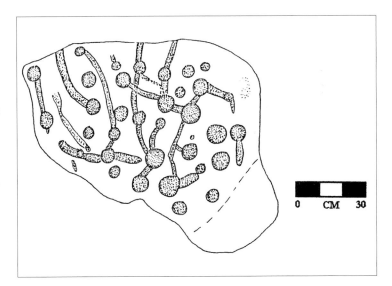

There is another factor to be taken into account when assessing the position of water sources: that modern drainage may have changed everything.

In more general terms, some motifs are found on rocks which occupy a significant place as a threshold. In Northumberland the sandstone scarps are dissected by streams that flow into the Milfield Plain and major panels look down on these streams or are at thresholds between the scarps and the plain, especially where the River Till breaks through at Weetwood Bridge (Beckensall 2001). The river is flanked for most of its northerly course (its name changes from Breamish to Till at Old Bewick) between sandstone scarps and ridges and glacial soils by panels of spectacular rock-art (Old Bewick, Amerside Law Moor, Chatton Park to the west and the Fowberry-Weetwood area to the west). When the river breaks through at Weetwood Bridge, it leaves the steep or undulating sandstone landscape to flow across the glacial sands and gravels of an ancient dried-up lake called Milfield (named after the Anglian site at Maelmin), where a concentration of henges, pits, burials, settlements and routeways has come to light, buried under the plough soil, with some now excavated. Here we have early settlement and 'ritual' sites from Mesolithic times onwards. The plain is overlooked by rock-art panels at Broomridge (ibid.). The rock-art at Roughting Linn lies close to a waterfall and undated multivallate enclosure ending at the cliff above it, linked to the Milfield Plain by a stream valley that is also flanked by an ancient trackway.

The coincidence of hills surrounding plains is clearly seen too in the landscape of the Kilmartin Glen (Beckensall 2005), with streams flowing to feed the River Add from areas rich in rock-art. A design at Creagantairbh, including an extended line, marks a threshold where the valley into the Kilmartin Glen narrows. Along another valley that joins it from the east is Torran where there are cups and cups-and-rings on a steep slope that ends at a loch. All around the narrow valleys penetrating the mountains are routeways punctuated by rock-art, such as at Glassvar. The routes lead through the valleys to lakes.

In the Lake District, the distribution of rock-art is particularly revealing, for the sites at Patterdale (Beckensall 2002) are concentrated in the valleys that provide the main lines of communication through the mountains, following the steep descent from the Kirkstone Pass.

Coastal areas attract rich rock-art, as we have seen in Ireland. In Galloway the concentration of motifs is in The Machars, the coastal lands, with some at specific inland sites connected with water. High Banks, for example, with its incredible use of well-made cups and concentric rings on outcrop, lies at a shallow dried-up lake or pond. Water, either as a source of communication for trade and contact further afield, or for watering animals, is of obvious value to prehistoric people.

55 Patterdale, Ullswater (C). The width of the rock here is 1.50m

56 High Banks, Galloway. *Jan Brouwer*

57 Stronach ridge, Arran

A special location for rock-art is on islands. In the Mediterranean, Malta, for example, has some of the world's oldest and impressively decorated temples, and underground sites. Islands have a special nature, more self-contained, perhaps allowing special developments to take place, but they can also be reached by boat, and people can reach other places from them. A good example of how a regional art form has developed is on the Isle of Arran; though not far from western peninsulas that are rich in rock-art it has only one major panel on outcrop at Stronach Ridge overlooking Brodick harbour to the east.

This extensive ridge is now obscured by planted forest, but even at the time when the rock-art was recorded in 1901 there were uninterrupted views all around, especially to the sea and the main mountains. When we speculate about whether rock-art was at clear view points at the time it was made, and consider that it may have been in forest clearings, we must also consider that the forest cover today may be recent. It is a curious concentration, as the main mass of concentrated prehistoric activity is at Machrie Moor, with its abundance of stone circles, none of which has any cup-marks. There are a few other isolated cup-marked rocks, but this large outcrop has an impressive number of 'keyhole-type' motifs. Why this should be is not known, but it is such a strong variant that one thinks of the local people developing this image with enthusiasm. Had they crossed the sea to Kintyre and Kilmartin, they would have seen many other variations, but obviously liked what they had created. The local archaeological society helped me with the recording, and I think that if there are more rock-art panels to be found, they will find them.

As these motifs are not well known, they deserve space in this book. Prehistoric motifs on a large expanse of outcrop on Stronach have been known since the late nineteenth century. The name itself ('nose-shaped') means a ridge. They were first observed by a shepherd c.1888, but were only recorded in some detail by the Rev J.E. Somerville during two visits to the island, when he 'removed a good deal of the turf with a spade, and this exposed a considerable surface' where the Old Red Sandstone slopes to the east in a divided north–south sheet. He wrote that the turf was thin at the top and thick at the bottom of the slope (0.46m). He noted the deep horizontal grooves as being 'perplexing, but they seem to be the result of weathering, or of running water'.

Mr Fred R. Coles then visited the site in May 1901, observing that tool marks in some of the motifs were distinct and that deeply-grooved channels running horizontally from north to south were water-worn and weathered. At the time of the survey the area was free of trees:

> It is some distance south and east of the actual Stronach ridge. There are several flat rock-surfaces in many directions at varying distances from the crest, but upon none could I trace any sculpturing whatever.

He noted, significantly, that on the crest of the ridge north-west of the motifs 'there seemed to me the remains of a cairn, much overgrown with heather'. The range of mountain peaks culminating in Ben Nuis was visible from the site, and presumably Brodick Bay.

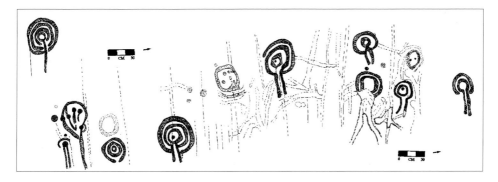

58 Stronach ridge: south-east part of the outcrop

Today the site is in a small woodland clearing in which the outcrop stands amid heather and grass. The top surface is overgrown. Any sense of its dominant position in the landscape is shut out by trees, except where the trackway allows a glimpse of Goat Fell.

The outcrop may be seen in two parts, divided east to west. The south part is a continuous sheet, sloping to the east, most of the motifs being on the bottom. The north part is a continuation of this, with motifs on the upper part and on an extension in the form of a sloping rectangle, separated from the main mass to the south.

Although there are variations on a theme, the main motif is a 'keyhole' – an apt description, as there is a circular boss either partially or completely surrounded by a ring or penannular (a gapped circle) from which two parallel grooves run. This basic motif may have additional concentric rings or penannulars. It is possible that the natural form of the rock, with its many parallel grooves running down, gave the idea for the parallels which echo it. It would have been easier to work on the lower slope to the south, as it is difficult to keep control of a hard stone pick whilst kneeling on a steep slope. This may account for the line of motifs concentrated there. The top of the northern rock presented no such difficulties; most of the figures are again in a horizontal line, below the natural oval depressions which may have been ice-scoured and possibly enhanced by people, although there are no visible pick-marks in them to prove this.

As with so many other sites in Britain, the Stronach site is desperately in need of a plan to assess the dangers to the rock, to decide how best to preserve it and how to present it to visitors. An area needs to be cleared around it, and the site displayed in such a way that people will be able to see the motifs without walking all over it and without churning up the muddy ground. There needs to be good signposting (at the moment non-existent), clear and firm access, and some tasteful display to show what is on the rock, and its importance. One need go no further than the Kilmartin Glen to see how this might be done.

More rock-art has come to light. As more people are aware of it, the more likely that other panels will be discovered. For example, there are two small flat 'portable' stones covered with cups now in the Heritage Centre, one found by a visitor at the entrance to the Drumadoon hillfort, where there is also a prominent standing stone. More art in the landscape is being recorded, including a destroyed burial structure, and a close look at standing stones may reveal more.

One warning, though: cup-marks present a particular problem on Arran, as geologically there are many natural ones, especially on the coastal sandstones, where holes like inverted cones are drilled by the sea.

The Isle of Man has rock-art, too. This was first gathered together by Ronald Morris (Morris 1979), and since then more has been found as a result of work by the University of Bournemouth. From a modest six stones, including Ballagawne Keill, Ballragh, a standing stone from Keill Vreeshey, and stones of unknown provenance in the Manx Museum, there are now over 50 sites listed, mostly with simple cup-marks, a few with more complex images, and – very significantly – some early 'hatchings' and animal figures (Darvill and O'Connor 2005), with surfaces as different as slate and granite. Among them are some incised 'sketches' that may include people carrying upturned boats, plausible for an island setting. More than 95 per cent are of the cup-and-ring type, with 50 per cent in the open-air, 30 per cent possibly from monuments and 20 per cent portable.

Seventy panels on fifty-five sites is a considerable increase that has come from intensive fieldwork, but the site that gives the article its name, Cronk yn How, suggests an interesting development that begins with a possible pair of standing stones demolished in the third millennium BC to allow a barrow to be built with a single central burial. Incised deer and lines may belong to the earlier use of the site.

The Orkney Islands has fine rock-art which stands among some of the finest and most concentrated prehistoric sites in Europe. Not only does it belong to destroyed and extant passage-graves, with emphasis on spirals, but there are many crossed hatchings that also occur as decoration on Neolithic houses. There is rock-art on other Scottish islands, which tends to concentrate on simple cup-marks.

Some of the greatest areas of art in the landscape have been so well documented (North-West Yorkshire, The North Yorkshire Moors and parts of Galloway) that I shall confine my comments to a few generalisations about their distribution.

For North-West Yorkshire, all the detail the reader may require is to be found in *Prehistoric Rock Art of the West Riding,* a well-researched survey by non-professional archaeologists inspired by curiosity and passion (Boughey and Vickerman 2003). From a recording of 297 marked rocks in 1986 it has expanded to 640. Ninety per cent of these lie in the watersheds of north Aire, north Wharfe, south Wharfe and south Washburn in a broad band on Millstone Grit east of the Pennine's anticline. It could be that agriculture has destroyed those on lower ground, as most lie in the 250m OD – 360m band. On the whole the motifs are simpler than those in roughly numerically-comparable areas, such as Northumberland or Galloway, with few really innovative designs, and there are few panels associated with monuments. Their distribution, however, is significant at extensive viewpoints and in clusters, not usually the highest points, on gently sloping ground. The research group adds new sites, with Nidderdale being most recent. There is within the limited symbolism of the panels some interesting

59 Westray, Orkney (now in
Kirkwall Museum)

variation which shows individual minds at work, and some of these panels have
become very well known and frequently illustrated. Among these are the 'ladder
motifs' and the complex linear patterns at Hanging Stone Ridge. One area of
landscape art became part of the English Heritage study in 2000, when the
recording of the motifs became a focal point for a comparison between laser
scanning and traditional rubbing methods. There was little to choose between
the results, both accurately showing what was on the rocks.

The North Yorkshire Moors area, though not having lots of marked rocks, has
a greater variety of contexts, ranging from those in, or associated with, burial
sites and at significant viewpoints. The Fylingdales area is an especially important
one, for the art is in places such as viewpoints, stream sources and possible
tracks. There is little outcrop but, like the Durham sites, there are many earthfast
boulders for them to decorate.

1 Loch Tay from the slopes of Ben Lawers, with rock 2 in the foreground. *P.M. Brown*

2 Graig Hill, south of Loch Tay (2006)

3 Kilmartin, Argyll, above the village, down the glen to Crinan. A line of four cairns is visible

4 The routeway at the Creag nam Braithrean site west of Kilmartin glen

5 A panel recorded in May 2006 on this routeway

Above: 6 Ballochmyle, Ayr. *Crown Copyright: RCAHMS*

Left: 7 Fylingdales, North Yorks Moors: a cup-marked slab, and cairn on the horizon

8 Osmond's Gill, Barningham Moor: a cup-and-ring slab lies among the scree on the right side

9 Ilkley Moor: Haystack Rock, Pancake Ridge

10 The Copt Howe massive decorated block, Cumbria, towards the Langdale Pikes. *P.M. Brown*

Opposite above: *11* Loughcrew cairns and landscape, Ireland

Opposite below: *12* Knowth, Ireland. Large and satellite cairns

Above: 13 Loughcrew passage-grave motifs

Left: 14 Long Meg

Right: 15 Balkemback, part of a stone setting, Angus

Below: 16 High Banks, Galloway, Scotland

17 Ballymeanoch, Kilmartin, Argyll

18 Blairbuie 2, Argyll, deep in a planted forest

19 Gayles Moor earthfast slab, Richmondshire, with part broken off

20 Buttony, Northumberland: pristine rock-art in an area that has not been well-managed

21 Fylingdales Moor

Opposite above: 22 Gallow Hill (Angus)

Opposite below: 23 Old Bewick, natural and artificial groves (N)

24 Castlebar, Ireland, 1999 presentation of a rubbing of the Bohea rock to the County library, with county and local historian officials present. *Tom Campbell Photography, Castlebar*

Above, opposite and overleaf: 25 Greenfield Community School art work by young people, that began with an encounter with prehistoric rock-art. *Sharon Simpson*

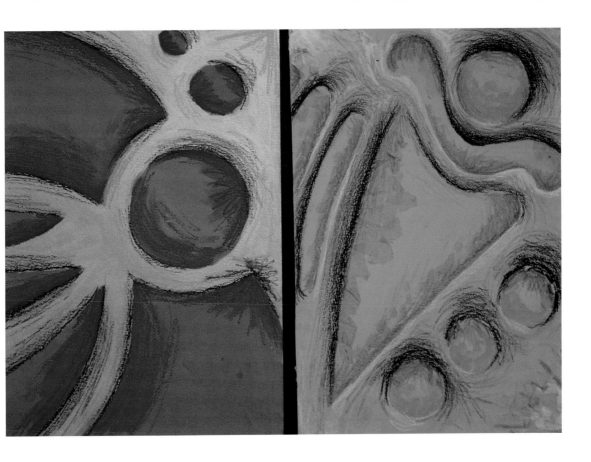

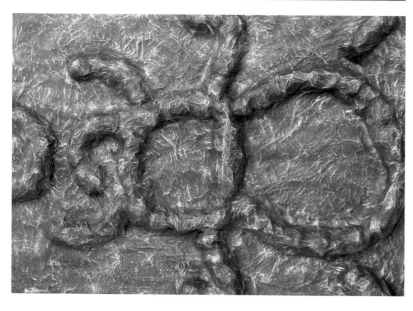

60 Ilkley view from the moor to the town

61 North Yorkshire Moors landscape: a cupped triangular slab is the the fore, with a cairn beyond

Ronald Morris published an account of the Galloway area in his pioneering work of 1979, but van Hoek has added considerably to the basis that he laid down. It is a pity that such a work should not be in a more sophisticated published form but nevertheless this is a very important survey, challenging someone or organisation to take it a stage further.

It is difficult to say whether *rock-shelter motifs* come under the heading 'landscape-art' or 'monuments'. Although rock-shelters are natural features, and are used all over Britain as shelters for prehistoric and later people, there are five known in Northumberland which are decorated in such a way that it adds considerably to their significance.

The rock-shelter at Corby's Crags (Beckensall 2001, 2003), excavated by the author, has already been fully documented. Here, a large ringed basin with a groove running from it down a large domed outcrop hangs over a space that has been used from Mesolithic to modern times, with an inverted Food Vessel full of cremation buried under a triangular slab on the floor, with a pecked groove running towards it.

Another, at Goatscrag Hill (ibid.) overhangs a floor that has been used for cremation burials in pits and pots of the Early Bronze Age, with four animal carvings, probably deer, but of no certain age, carved into the vertical wall inside the shelter. On the overhang there are cups linked with curved grooves, like horseshoes. The whole ridge, of which the shelter forms part, has panels of rock-art leading via destroyed burial sites to the Milfield Plain in the west, and to the Roughting Linn site in the east, all at extensive viewpoints.

Ketley Crag (ibid.) is the latest and most spectacular discovery. When I first recorded this decorated floor with its overhang there was only a strip of the design showing, but persons unknown uncovered most of the rest; the final uncovering, the eastern strip, was made necessary when a wandering cow disturbed the grass at the edge. So there have been three successive drawings. The shelter, with a view across a wide stream valley to the range of Cheviot Hills, lies in an area of many skilfully-decorated rock panels and others, again part of a succession of viewpoints.

Another, at Cartington Cove, near Rothbury, known to contain art without any further record, was blown up. Cuddy's Cave, Dod Law, so-named because it was thought to be one of the resting places for St Cuthbert's body to its final burial place at Durham, has recorded rock-art, some of it prehistoric, though this has been eroded. Many other rock-shelters in the county have been explored, with finds of flints from Mesolithic times onwards, but so far without any more rock-art having been found.

It is now at last possible to add cave-art to the rock-shelters, this time at Creswell Crags, near Worksop, putting the earliest rock-art into the Upper Palaeolithic period, about 13,000 years ago. The discoveries are not Lascaux-

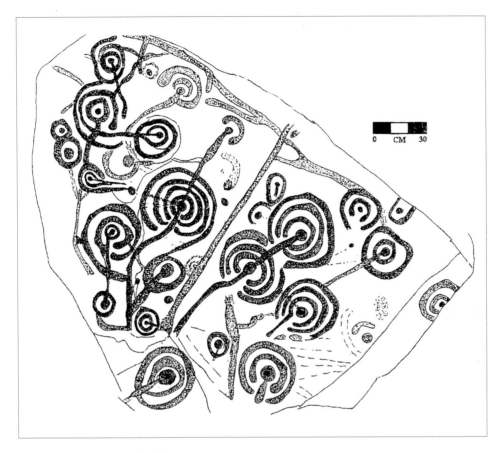

62 Ketley Crag (N): the third drawing

like, and are faintly-made incisions depicting animals. The caves have been long known for being habitations for prehistoric people, and there was already a collection of excavated material, when Paul Bahn and his colleagues set out in earnest to examine all the interior rock faces among the caves that face a long rift in the limestone. The result: dozens of engravings of animals to add to the bones excavated in the 1870s: bones of hyena, mammoth and bison, with stone and bone tools; at the time two engraved bones were found, until that time the only figurative art known in Britain. Some of the engravings are superimposed with other prehistoric art but also with unfortunate modern graffiti. Bird forms, stags, and others have been found by applying oblique lighting to the cave walls systematically, and it is an incredible part of the story that the explorers were about to leave the caves thinking there was nothing there, when the first image was seen (CA 197, 2005). From small beginnings, the site now has an impressive museum and storage facilities for all the artefacts.

63 Creswell Crags: stag with the graffiti. *Paul Bahn*

After these discoveries, the University of Bristol Speleological Society examined a site called Aveline's Hole in Somerset, known for its Upper Palaeolithic and Mesolithic artefacts, and discovered a panel 25cm wide by 20cm high, with incised lines that cross to form lozenges. Those who discovered it consider it to be Mesolithic, but this type of motif is commonly found in passage-graves (ibid.).

There is an important extension of places where people are looking for rock-art, and it is appropriate if I end this brief survey with a look at new rock-art discoveries in Angus, around Tealing.

All the marked rocks occupy south-facing intermediate hill slopes, not the high part of the hills, and above the fertile plain below. The motifs are on slabs and earthfast-boulders. The lower area has seen various cists uncovered, generally in the nineteenth century, some superficially buried, some on tops of natural hillocks, as a result of ploughing and gravel extraction. Of some, little or nothing is known; others have skeletal remains and cremations, with worked flints, urns and Food Vessels of the Early Bronze Age. These generally lie below the sites where the most recent rock-art discoveries have been made, the latter commanding wide views across the landscape in all directions but the north where the line of hills rises.

There now follows an examination of each new site.

Gallow Hill 1, found in 2003, is a slab of compact sandstone with some iron staining and lies above a recent quarry, around which is a scatter of similar, unmarked slabs. As pick-marks are clearly visible and fresh, it is likely that this rock has not been exposed for long, either because it was buried or was lying face down, possibly as a cist cover. It is not likely to be in situ, but may be close to its original location. Most of the surface is decorated, and the design appears to fit the shape of the rock. It is a complex arrangement of cups, curved, circular and oval grooves, with connections between individual motifs that make the design fluid. Outstanding, especially in oblique light, are symmetrical, quite deep cup-marks, the largest of which has a distinct inverted cone profile and clear pick-marks. The largest cups lie at the centre of concentric rings and ovals, the smaller forming a line of an arc or connected by grooves to run down the rock on the left. Some small cups are embedded in the circular and oval grooves, and may have been there first. Two parallel oval grooves include straight sections and enclose two linked cups. At the top of the rock there are two large cups surrounded by three rings each which runs into the other at the place where the motifs meet, the left one being dominant. Both have cups included in their rings. The outer ring of the right-hand side motif runs to the edge of the slab. To the left of these joined motifs are five cups connected by curved grooves.

The motifs in the lower left-hand corner are not so clear. The main image is a cup at the centre of two roughly circular grooves that merge to make one. The outer groove impinges on the oval, and is probably later in date. There are some faint parallel grooves running from the oval from left to right, enclosed at the top by a groove that runs through a cup. There are some very faint lines running from top to bottom, one of which links up with an arc surrounding a cup outside the conjoined double circles. The contrast between deep, bold picking and the more tentative, fainter grooves, is only evident in good light conditions.

Gallow Hill has a large number of cairns, some only *c*.1m diameter; some of these could be for field clearance, but others may be for burials. Their function is not always clear unless they have been excavated, as some have been in the past.

Gallow Hill 2 is a decorated earthfast slab that lies at a slightly lower level than Gallow Hill 1 (above) on a small terrace. To the west is a steep valley. The site commands an all-round view of the landscape except to the north. The near-horizontal sandstone slab has almost all its surface covered with well-made cups, four of which are linked with grooves like a string of beads. Six cups have a single ring, one a penannular, and another has an arc. One cup has a curved

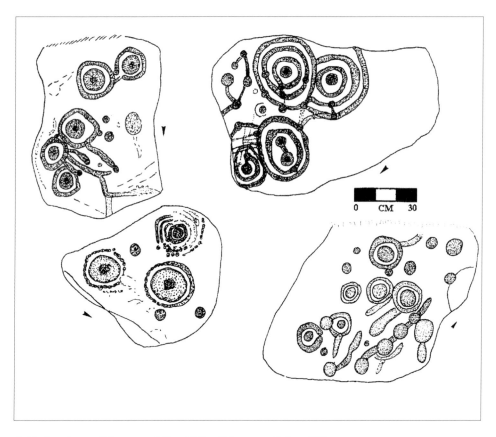

64 Tealing, Angus: Prieston 2, Gallow Hill 1, Prieston 1, Gallow Hill 2

groove running from it. None of the ringed cups has a groove running from it; five have grooves running from the ring.

The Prieston earthfast boulders are on the lowest slopes of the hill and lie close to a derelict Second World War building connected with an airfield to the south. They lie in an area of permanent grass and gorse, with a deep hollow-way running in from the north.

Prieston 1 is a large, compact, rounded sandstone, one of many in the area, and lies behind gorse. Triangular in shape, its prominent feature is a large, deep pick-marked basin surrounded closely by a single ring. The basin narrows at its base, forming an inverted cone shape. A slightly smaller basin lies at the apex of the triangle. Four cups form unlinked corners of a rectangle around the larger basin, one surrounded by faint pecked-in concentric rings. There is a plough scratch *c.*20cm long.

Prieston 2 is either a large embedded boulder or part of the bedrock. It is a compact sandstone with its motifs in pristine condition, indicating little or no exposure. The design is likely to be complete, as the long groove that runs into a lower level of stone terminates. On the upper part are two deep cups, inverted cones, with single rings, one joining the other, but leaving a small gap. A more complex arrangement lies at the lower-left corner, with three deep cups in an arc at the centre of grooves that are more or less circular, and touch. The largest, with an angular groove, has a groove running from it to a cup. The central cup-and-ring has three grooves that lead away from the ring: a central groove that runs down the rock changing direction in a branch before continuing with a lightly-pecked area before it stops. On either side of this central groove are grooves that curve upwards, ending in cups and making a 'keyhole' shape. The lower groove runs through the ring that surrounds the third cup. Two cups lie outside this groove, and small one. There is an oval to the right of these cups, deeper on one side, with pick-marks visible.

The motifs follow the general gentle slope of the rock, and the main five cups lie in an arc that occupies over half the surface. There is a distinctive flow in the design and connection, similar to the Gallow Hill 1 rock, giving the impression that they were in the same general tradition.

A large flat-topped block/boulder at Tealing Hill Wood is one of many in a line along the edge of a cleared field before it drops away to an area of broad medieval-type rig and furrow. First reported by Romilly Allen in the late nineteenth century, it then lay in a wood (hence the name).

It is one of many boulders that could have been selected for marking, all of which may have been moved during field-clearance to the edge. To the east is a well-surfaced old trackway and a redundant land-fill site, grown over. There are two standing stones here, supposedly part of a 'four-poster' setting, with extensive views over the lower ground.

The block, roughly triangular, has its top, slightly-sloping surface marked with an additional cup on the near-vertical south-west face. It is roughly divided lengthways by a natural crack/depression that has been further exploited, as most of the motifs cluster on either side of it at the centre and north end. The motifs are not easy to see, as it is partly eroded; the 16 cups mostly have rings or arcs around them, most not complete.

Further investigation by Romilly Allen showed that other decorated rocks had been found and lost. He listed a collection of Mr M'Nicoll of three stones with cups found on Tealing Hill 'on the site of primitive dwellings near Tealing' and in a stackyard wall; all have gone. At Cross House, Balkemback, a stone built into the north-west corner has 13 cups, some deep, all now covered with pebbledash. Another two stones were found near Achterhouse, 5 miles west of Tealing at the foot of the hill. One had many cups and one cup and arc; the other had similar but fewer marks.

Above: 65 Tealing, Angus: a possible cist slab on the edge of a quarry

Left: 66 Tealing, Prieston 2. *George Currie*

Other reports in the same area of cists, bones, cremations and pottery are but a glimpse of what was in the region in prehistory, but it helps us to see rock-art not in isolation but as part of a wider picture. It is only by relating it to such finds that we can begin to understand some of its purpose.

Further afield, George Currie's other discoveries are in a wider prehistoric landscape. At The Hill of Menmuir two marked rocks lie in a very interesting prehistoric landscape of enclosures, field systems and cairns. The site is north-west of Brechin, south-south-west of White Catherun hillfort (enclosing cup-marked stones), on the 220m OD contour. Located at the bottom of a large grass field, one outcrop slab has three clear cups and, unusually, a cup on a narrow vertical ledge, dropping away to the rest of the buried outcrop.

67 Gallow Hill: view over lowland, with George Currie sitting by one of his discoveries

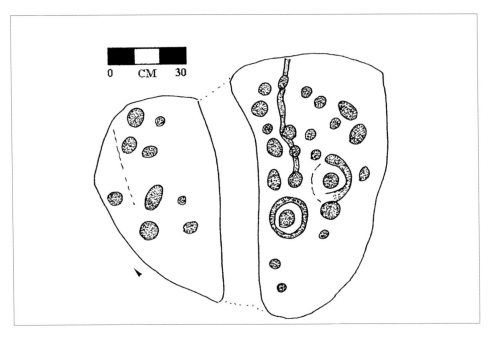

0   CM   30

68 Hill of Menmuir

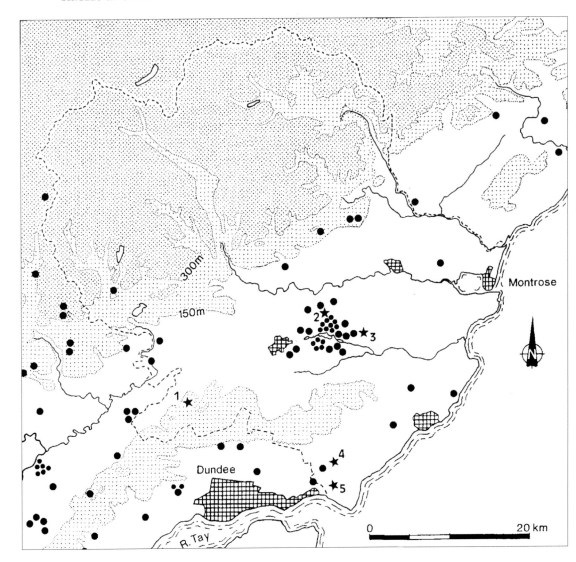

69 Angus and Fife distribution map of marked rocks. *John Sherriff, Crown Copyright: RCAHMS*

The second rock is sloping outcrop, rather like an open book, as there are two levels. Both faces of the sloping outcrop are decorated. The site lies among scattered cairn material, mainly cobbles, and is flanked by a stone and earth dump wall that is straight higher up the field, then curves like a snake down to the bottom.

The east face has 17 separate cups. Four others are linked to each other with grooves like a string of beads. There is a cup and complete ring and a cup and arc. The grooves follow the downward slope. The west face has eight cups of different sizes.

There is an excellent record and summary of rock-art in Angus and adjacent areas, of which the above are additions, by John Sherriff in *The Tayside and Fife Archaeological Journal* (Vol. 1 1995, Vol. V 1999) entitled *Prehistoric rock-carving in Angus*, in which new discoveries have been added to those made by people like Romilly Allen, whose recording was mainly centred on Forfar. There is an even bigger concentration there now, and Sherriff's new distribution map includes Neolithic small finds.

At first Neolithic distribution patterns related to settlements indicated by finds of stone axes, carved stone balls and other portable artefacts, but aerial photography has been able to discover more. The rock-art distribution does not accord closely with Neolithic settlement pattern or concentrations of small finds. Perhaps they are of a different period or belong to people whose life-style was different. Sherriff has commented that 'they have a national relevance in constituting the largest and densest concentration of rock-art out-with (outside) the highland area of Scotland' (Sherriff 1995). Since then he has added more to the record, and no doubt a combination of professional and independent archaeologists will add many more in the future.

In Argyll one has to continue to look beyond the now-famous rock-art panels in the area immediately bordering Kilmartin Glen to higher ground and more inaccessible places, where we are noting more passes and routeways leading to the Glen and its feeder streams. As recently as May 2006, for example, we discovered a flat panel of well-made cups above a stream bed leading to lower ground, at Creag nam Braithrean with extensive views from it across the glen (NR82057 99043) (Beckensall and Brown forthcoming) (*colour plates 3* and *4*). The coast of Loch Fyne has also revealed more to the south of Lochgair, at East Kames: two boulders with cups-and-rings at high viewpoints. Clearly, there is much more rock-art to discover and record all over Britain.

6

Art in burials and other monuments

The occurrence of art in burials and on standing stones is widely-spread, but thin on the ground, and is the best chance we have of establishing a timescale for its use. It demonstrates that the tradition of decoration takes place over hundreds of years, during which time its *origins* may have been incomprehensible to the people who continued to use the motifs in specialised contexts, and in a different way. There is, however, continuity in the kinds of motifs chosen, many common to all periods, especially the humble cup-mark. However they were used, there appears to be a compulsion to use symbols and motifs and a conviction about their efficacy.

Their use ranges from Orkney, where some of the finest British spiral motifs are located, to a megalithic tomb at Tregiffian where cup-marks on its entrance, now visible, were once hidden inside the Neolithic tomb until its reconstruction in the Early Bronze Age, and into the Channel Islands. The ritual of making the marks also extends to the deposit of cup-marked stones in settlement sites, one buried under the floor of a Middle Bronze Age house at Trethellan Farm, Newquay, Cornwall (Nowakowski 1991).

Sometimes the marked stones are literally carried over from one monument to another, perhaps a symbolic act of capturing the power of one place and transferring it to another. In which case we have to be careful not to try to date the monument from this addition, but it does underline a sense of continuity. A good example of this process is seen in a recent excavation at *Balblair*, near Inverness, which will be described later. Other recent excavations will be used to ask how far they have brought us closer to an explanation of their use in burials, and when. To begin with, I take the oldest in the tradition and some of the most spectacular examples of rock-art.

Left: 70 An example of passage-grave art in Brittany

Above: 71 Motifs in the Gavrinis passage-grave, France, are similar to those in the Irish passage-graves, suggesting a strong connection

PASSAGE–GRAVE ART

There are several kinds of monuments in Ireland, the most famous being the passage-graves/chambered-tombs in the bend of the Boyne: Dowth, Newgrange and Knowth, where there are also two henges, a cursus, and some standing stones (I).

The outstanding position of passage-grave art in Britain is highlighted by the fact that Knowth alone contains over a quarter of Europe's megalithic rock-art with 300 large stones in the main mound, although it is smaller than Newgrange. The repertoire of motifs is so like that in Brittany that a contact between the two areas by sea is almost certain, possibly from Brittany to Ireland. From Ireland we have some offshoots of similar art in Anglesey.

It isn't only motifs that are shared with Europe, for the practice of choosing certain kinds of stone for the construction of tombs, in some cases brought at great effort over sea and land, and the choice of special stone for objects like axes, often won from inaccessible and dangerous places, is also common. To share the concepts of megalithic architecture among regions is as important as sharing motifs. A deliberate placing of motifs at significant places in the tomb structure, either at the entrance, in the passage or in the chambers to which they lead, is recognised. They are also placed around the mound, on the kerbstones. In Ireland the symbols and motifs take the form of cup-and-ring marks, cups, and more specialised use of parallel, crossed and serpentine grooves, lozenges, chevrons and spirals of different kinds, which are present in other non-passage-grave areas, but not in such profusion or elaboration.

We tend to know and remember particularly fine panels of carefully-contained art filling the whole surface of the rock, but there are many more motifs, some hidden, that look more like the beginning of such designs, far more sketchy. The reason is one that I have always held: that the act of making a motif was significant, and that it did not have to be 'finished' or combined with others to form a complete panel. Panels covered with art are much rarer, and as such seem more impressive to us. Even on the kerbs, it is interesting to see how many motifs seem random and incomplete. Not only the act of making them was important; they would have been recognised for their significance by the people who viewed them. It was a great physical effort to move all those stones into position, having transported many of them for miles, so why not complete the job and make all decoration to the highest standard? Here we are looking at it from a modern point of view; we must not make such assumptions.

It is easy enough for us in our study to isolate symbols and motifs and to draw up a repertoire. It is also possible to separate those that are sketched out with incised lines before being worked on with a pick, and to show that some incised lines did not lead to finished designs made by pecking out the stone using a harder stone. We have to distinguish between those that appear to be complete from those we *assume* to be incomplete without putting too much importance on which were more highly regarded at the time. In the case of Newgrange, the most elaborate and complete are at crucial places. The entrance stone is obviously a work of art by any standards. Similarly, the kerbstone opposite the entrance is remarkable for the organisation of motifs and for the division between two different concepts of the use of motifs in design. Both of these stones have these divisions, the line in the entrance stone running into a spiral. Is this a gap, a division or an opening? Like the entrance itself or like the division between those allowed in and those outside? Is it like the crack in W.H. Auden's teacup that opens 'a lane to the land of the dead'? The box arrangement over the entrance which allows the sun's rays to penetrate at the winter solstice has the crossed lines that denote entrances on this and other mounds' lintels.

72 Newgrange façade

The three joined spirals along the passage are not unique as a design, for they are found on the cliff face at Morwick (N) and at Achnabreck (K), but they are unique in passage-grave art, and may indicate a special place. As in other tombs, there is a decorated basin, a focal point in the chamber, that must have been meant to hold something, like bones, ash, dried flowers or herbs, or liquid, but who knows for sure? The idea of offering to someone or something is there. If we were to know nothing about such things, the font bowl in a church would be thought of as a receptacle, but a knowledge of the rite that went with it, the symbols of deliverance from slavery across the Red Sea, of being born again, of moving through cleansing from darkness to light and of being accepted through this act into a community of worshippers, would be unknown.

The passage floor rises naturally from entrance to chambers, where it is possible to stand upright, to fit in some visitors perhaps, and to conduct ceremonies there such as laying the dead to rest.

Above is a corbelled ceiling, elaborately decorated on a cap that forms the base of the flat mound above. It is right to think of this as an important feature; a dome up to the heavens? We have entered from the domestic world outside, most familiar to us, been restricted by the sides of a passage along which we have travelled, shut in, perhaps in an eerie silence in a cave-like world, and in the chamber the dome reminds us that we will see the light again. Now you

73 Newgrange three spirals. The spiral pattern is 28cm high and 30cm across. *Ronald Morris*

might want to think of this as a cosmos in which we move from one region to another, from profundity to level earth, to sky. This is a process common to all the passage-graves. A journey from darkness to light *may be* a journey of revelation, one in which we metaphorically and in reality see light at the end of the tunnel, peace after a conflict, a light of hope shining in the darkness. We bring our own words and experiences to try to understand what it meant to the original builders. We pass through a deliberately-created space where we can be awed, made silent, shut in, forced to think inwardly. For some it could be an initiation into a different world.

The presence of bones in chambers under the mound adds another factor: that the ancestors are there. In reality these are their remains, but these bones and ash can be thought of as *them*. The skull that Hamlet holds is not just the dead jester, Yorik, but a reminder of what a lovable character he was in his lifetime. He lives again in recollection and in imagination. Ancestors are with us, not only in our genes, but in what they have helped to build, a visible presence of fields, buildings, walls and memories.

The mound at Knowth is smaller than Newgrange, but it has two entrances opposite each other almost meeting in the middle of the mound. Before the tomb, as with the others, there was earlier Neolithic activity from *c.*3900-3500 BC, when people lived in circular houses. This was a mixed-farming community

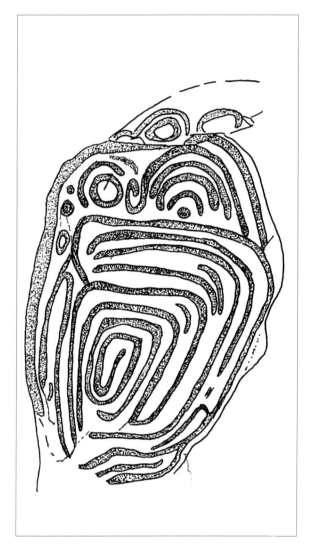

Left: 74 Knowth 'ghostly guardian'

Above: 75 The 'ghostly guardian'
is similar in concept to the
arrangement of symbols in the
Gavrinis passage-grave, France

when settlement began to replace a more mobile way of life, although mobility
continued with the grazing and hunting of animals further afield. The tombs are
evidence that some places in the landscape have great significance and power
to the settlers, dwarfing the domestic buildings and requiring an expenditure of
energy and time. This activity lasted until *c.*2500 BC, and rock-art played a strong
part in its expression (*colour plate 12*).

Knowth is different from Newgrange in that it is surrounded by 18 other
small passage tombs, with their entrances facing the great mound arranged like
a giant clock face. It is possible that these aligned radiating passages could be
represented by compositions that look like sundials. The archaeologists who have

excavated these mounds recently have not written purely impersonal accounts of their discoveries; some of their reports are heavy with wonder about what they discovered: the past speaking eloquently to the future. It is when a sense of wonder leaves archaeologists that it is time to give up. One particular orthostat half-way down the west passage resembled for Professor Eogan 'an anthropo-morphic figure with two large staring eyes ... a ghostly guardian'.

If it had this effect on him, then it was likely to have had a great impact too on the prehistoric beholders. It was not necessarily designed to look human, but 'how easily is a bush supposed to be a bear' in a tunnel with only a faint light, when pressure of darkness and confinement may alter our consciousness. The Abbe Breuil saw human faces and forms in many different kinds of rock-art, but he found what he was looking for. In this stone many common symbols are used, expressed in a unique combination, with concentric 'angular' spirals, concentric or 'nested' arcs, border and circles.

Again, the basin is a dominant feature in the eastern chamber, but a suggestion that the tomb may have been built around it is speculative. Why not just bring it in when the tomb was completed, as a finishing touch? The significance of it as a basin is that it is circular and lies in a circular tomb, an echo of the whole place.

The kerbstones at Knowth are more impressive generally then those at Newgrange, originally 127 of them, built in such a way that their tops were level, starting at the entrances and becoming smaller the further away they are. The motifs are varied, and may have been marked and erected by different people in groups. This idea of different working groups being responsible for the construction of part of a mound or monument is not uncommon. Our excavation of the large Neolithic/Early Bronze Age cairn at Blawearie (N) that was kerbed by a continuous ring of standing stones demonstrated different techniques in the erection of small groups of stones.

There is a range of motifs including spirals, concentric uncupped rings, serpentine grooves, diffuse pecking, and long ovals containing circles, and arcs and radials. The art draws on a fund of symbols and motifs. Of special interest are the entrance stones at Knowth which have a similar division laterally to those at Newgrange, and may be seen to indicate an entrance. Whether you want to see this also as a 'cosmological entrance' is another matter.

Another notable feature at Knowth and Newgrange is the incorporation of quartz into the building material. This gives the Newgrange façade its glaring white approach from the river. It is thought that quartz crystals have mystic properties with these powers valued to such an extent that the wearing of such crystals today gives people reassurance. It is also a white, hard rock that can be used for tool-making and for engraving on rock surfaces. In Sussex, in the

76 Knowth kerbstone

Central Weald, I excavated a 19m-diameter round barrow of the Early Bronze Age in which the centre was enclosed by two concentric circles of sandstones cemented together by a thick compact white sand with layers in it suggesting that it had been brought in by the basketful (Beckensall 1967). The effect of this was to form a white interior collar. At the time of excavation this was the only known barrow in the Central Weald; the majority of burials were on the chalk Downs, where they would have contrasted sharply with the surrounding vegetation. Perhaps those who built 'Money Mound' were imitating what they thought of as the norm.

What is even more interesting is that the quartz had been brought by sea or land from the Wicklow Mountains, 38 miles away. The marked rocks that made up the mound structure were sandstone (Greywacke), carried in from a few miles north. This transporting of stones for specific purposes is also seen in the bluestones of Stonehenge, but it is also seen in the choice of 'exotic' stone for the manufacture of high-quality polished axes, a must-have for so many people, suggesting that the stone itself had special meaning, especially as many of the axes found show no signs of wear. What Newgrange shows us is that stone was used according to a plan, not randomly chosen. Notice how Long Meg (C) is made of red Eden Valley Sandstone, covered with motifs, and lying outside the entrance to a circle made of volcanic glacial erratics.

The well-publicised 'macehead' of superbly-carved flint with motifs of mainly spirals flowing from surface to surface was found in the east passage at Knowth, lying in front of a stone basin and covered with shale. Its horned and other spiral designs are echoed in open-air rock-art at Morwick (N) and Achnabreck (K), Temple Wood stone circle (K) and in a presumed Neolithic pit grave with layers of cremation at Lilburn (N).

As the interiors of these graves are so profusely covered with motifs, one asks whether different designs meant different things, and I find that impossible to answer, for I cannot enter the minds of the people who designed them. I can understand the concept of rows of stone planted upright to form a passage, roofed, some of them with arrangements to drain water away from the passage, leading into chambers where arrangements were made to honour the dead. I can understand the sheer sense of conviction that led people to expend so much energy on them, perhaps to the neglect of some pressing domestic tasks, I can understand the pride that they must have felt as they stood or walked around to view it. I can see a social elite pleased that it has once more stamped its authority on the land and the people. The dark places in the tombs could well have been a place for prophecy, perhaps of magnified voices echoing in the chambers, often manipulative to keep them in power. The rock-art was not secret or exclusive, as it appeared also on the outside of the tomb on the kerbstones. Its images may even have been present in tattoos on the skin, on leather or on wood. The use of symbolism is an intensely human experience to be shared, and is not confined to British rock-art. I can agree with Lewis-Williams that:

Architecture and art thus coalesced to represent, facilitate and induce religious experience, belief and practice. (Lewis-Williams 2005)

It has always been so.

There are some who like to think of prehistoric religion as 'sun worship', but there is no evidence here for that. Neither do we need to accept a precisely-worked-out geometric pattern for Neolithic architecture based on the heavens. Of course Newgrange has a box above the entrance which admits the sun directly down the passage at the winter solstice, and Stonehenge is aligned on the same phenomenon, but any suggestion that in some way a priesthood controlled people with predicted eclipses is fantasy. Neither did people need a calendar for the farming year; they lived closer to nature than anyone, and could read all the signs for themselves. We all know the life-giving properties of sun, earth, rain, and all hope that they will work for us, or even pray for them when they are particularly needed. We seek all kinds of controls to ensure that our lives are fruitful, and the expressions of wish-fulfilment, fortified by the use of symbols for hundreds of years, may be embodied in marks on the rocks. Rock-art is an integral part of the meaning of the monuments.

You may want to see it in this way:

> We add that altered states of consciousness and parallels with the structure went hand in hand with these distinctions. Power resides in control of consciousness in transition through the cosmos, and was epitomised by megalithic monuments. (Ibid.)

I leave readers to think out for themselves what that means.

States of consciousness, altered by drugs in documented examples of people still living in communities not completely swamped by the modern world, and of those that have been well documented historically, have been the subject of scientific experiments that have led to this exploration of the subconscious. Today we see a quite different use of drugs, including alcohol, that is so releasing that it threatens the very fabric of modern society to the extent that fundamentalist groups that do not go along that path need only to wait for the collapse of the societies that they hate from the inside, supported by an increasing flow of drugs from the outside. This is quite a different scenario from the controlled opening of the doors of perception that scientists explore in their attempts to understand the human mind. One approach leads some to the conclusion that:

> Religion is, ultimately, embedded in neurology, as is pre-scientific cosmology; the two are hardly separate. We have argued that, fundamentally, religion is based on belief in supernatural realms and non-material entities. Perceptions of those invisible realms derive from the electro-chemical function of the brain. (Ibid.)

The statistical basis for this premise was provided in close relationship to a study of the passage-graves by Jeremy Dronfield (Dronfield 1996), who wanted to know whether a diagnosis of the shapes and patterns of motifs was associated with altered states of consciousness. He began with motifs common in all abstract art, and with elements wired into the nervous system (such as arcs, spirals, U-shapes, filigrees) revealed in laboratory experiments in which the people affected by mind-altering drugs were asked to draw what they saw. Working with five groups of passage-graves where there was a reliably full range of motifs, he found a significant match with the 'entoptic' images deep in the brain. When he examined the position of these images in the tombs he found that each motif had a meaning or meanings, which in turn governed where they would be placed on stone. The spiral was particularly important, as he saw this as the vortex, a tunnel image, a route to a life beyond this, a contact with another world, including that of ancestors, Concentric images were mostly connected with the passage, as the viewer looked along it. At Loughcrew, as elsewhere, the passage is associated with curved concentric motifs, whereas lattices were found to be mostly in the chambers.

Out of the hundreds of passage-graves in Ireland and elsewhere very, very few of them contain motifs, so we must be careful not to label the few as typical. The same applies to the incidence of rock-art in later cairns. Why should this be? There may be many more motifs to be revealed in excavations and re-excavations, but even so this great absence is puzzling. Was there something so special about the sites singled out for decoration? If so what? So many people write as though there are many decorated rocks in the landscape, but even in the areas where there are the greatest concentrations, the number is small. So we can only write about the few we know and to draw some conclusions from them.

An offshoot of the Boyne valley sites is on the island of Anglesey, in easy reach by sea, where only two passage-graves have motifs. The architecture of the two mounds shows that they are smaller versions of the Boyne tombs, and both have spirals as part of their decoration. Spirals do not exclusively mean 'passage-grave art' as some people assume, as these also appear in the open-air.

One is called Bryn Celli Dhu, inland, where the sequence of events as far as we can understand them points to a curious inversion of monument building, for the mound is built at the centre of an earlier henge. Normally, henges are built later, in the late Neolithic/Early Bronze Age, some hundreds of years later. The henge was built on a small natural rise: a ditch with an outer wall enclosing a circle of 14 standing stones, focused perhaps on a central pit in which there may have been a stone or wooden post. A passage-grave built over the centre, leaving the ditch, was covered with a mound possibly constructed from the wall around the ditch. Some of the standing stones were deliberately broken up and incorporated in the mound. A kerb was built around it, which had the practical value of holding in the cairn stones, and emphasising the importance of the circle. Whereas henges were built as open-air ritual sites, with an occasional deposit of bone, the tomb that followed it was for burial. A slight curve in the kerb leads to the entrance, and a passage leads from there to a polygonal chamber in which there is a standing stone, not propping anything up, but freestanding and profusely decorated with serpentine grooves and spirals on its top and two of the sides. Behind the chamber was a pit that had been dug and filled in, marking the centre of the henge. Could the decorated stone have come from that pit? Possibly, but whether the decoration was already on it or added at the same time as the building of passage and chamber is not known.

The mound of Barclodiad y Gawres, an apronful of stones spilt there by a giantess (or in other mounds by the Devil), is a relatively modern mythological name for a large reconstructed mound that stands on land overlooking the Irish Sea, visible from that sea. It is a passage with a repertoire of motifs on seven slabs built into it. When I first recorded the rock-art in this tomb, a process that took many hours, I did so without much light, but with wax on paper, as a result of which I actually recorded more than I saw at the time of my first entrance (Beckensall 1999 and 2002), and since then another series of faint chevron designs has been found on a seventh rock. After notice of this appeared on the Internet, Nash recorded faint vertical and horizontal lines forming a chevron (Nash *et al.* 2006). Five of my recorded rocks have spirals; they begin at the chamber end of the passage and, with others that are unmarked, enclose the centre of the chamber. On the western side of the end of the passage is a horizontal stone decorated with chevrons, concentric lozenges, and with concentric serpentine grooves similar in effect to those on the Bryn Celli Dhu standing stone. Excavation has not answered all the questions about its use, but it does seem primarily or solely for burial. There was a curious stew found in the centre consisting of many creatures including frog, natterjack toad, snake, shrew, rabbit, mouse, eel and whiting, presumably not for human consumption and more like the contents of the Weird Sisters' cauldron, but apart from incorporating things from the outside world into the place of the dead, we can only speculate about its significance or purpose.

In England the six Calderstones (Forde-Johnson 1957) share passage-grave art traditions. They came from a megalithic tomb on the north side of the Mersey, but have been moved from their original location to Liverpool for their safety.

The tradition of using rock-art in monuments extends to sites other than those already mentioned in Wales, which now has a total of 33 recorded sites with nearly 40 panels, mostly on the fringes of the central uplands, with many on the north-west coast and others along the major river valleys of east Glamorgan and the southern Marches. Although the predominant motifs on Irish passage-graves have been described, other monuments do not share 'exotic' motifs, but have simple cups. These monuments are not the round barrows where cups and cups-and-rings usually occur.

In Wales, at Bachwen there is a capstone on a megalithic tomb with 110 cups and some grooves. It has been observed (Darvill and Wainwright 2003) that 'over one-third of the 28 recorded cup-mark dominated panels in Wales are monument based', and that 'none of the panels carrying passage-grave art in Wales also carry motifs associated with the cup-mark style'.

A portal dolmen in County Tyrone, at Ballyrenan (Davies 1937), is similar in type to the Welsh Dyffryn Ardudwy, Merioneth portal dolmen, which has cups on the north portal of the west chamber (Lynch 1969, p.131). The capstone of another megalithic tomb has two triangular hollows on top of its capstone. At Trefaes Moylgrove the possible capstone of a portal-dolmen has 28 cups and 17 depressions.

This exploration of the significance of rock-art in megalithic tombs has drawn attention to all kinds of theories and problems, but the examples do show what a significant place it held on some sites. Excavation continues in some of them, but a continuation of an investigation begun in the late 1970s at Carrowmore in County Sligo in north-west Ireland by a Swedish team led by Goran Burenhult has revealed the first decorated rock-art there: at *Lisoghil* (tomb 51), in the centre of the cemetery, a 35m-diameter cairn had a cist under a flat limestone roof slab with circular carvings on the front side of the roof slab. It was partially excavated from 1996-8, and carbon-dating placed the tomb to around 3550 BC, but it was significantly used long before that, suggested by a destroyed megalithic construction beneath it. The startling conclusion of the excavator is that evidence points to the use of the cemetery site long before that of the Boyne valley tombs, with carbon dates indicating a late Mesolithic, early Neolithic date for its beginning. Other archaeologists are wading in with questions about the validity of the carbon dates, so there will be a lively debate ahead (CA 2005). The motifs in question are three arcs joined, two of them doubled up with concentric arcs, and a small circle and arc.

Not all rock-art in passage-graves is as spectacular as that in Ireland. For example, in 1998, Richard Bradley's team recorded the scratched lines formed by zigzags, triangles and lozenges in Maes Howe on Orkney, with special lighting and great patience, forming a link between these markings and those already noted on houses and other architecture of the Neolithic. Again, it is interesting to note what others have missed, despite a site like Maes Howe having been

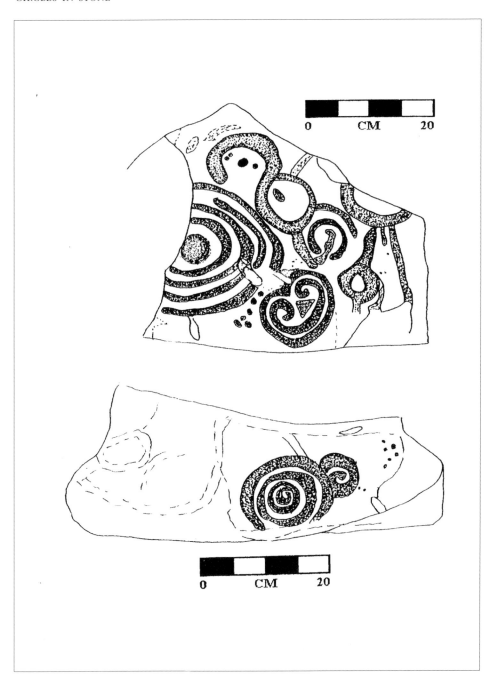

77 Lilburn (N) from a pit grave

visited and researched for many years. There is more awareness now of what to look for.

Some of the finest British rock-art comes from Orkney, at sites listed in *British Prehistoric Rock Art* (Beckensall 1999, 2002b, pp.115-6). The spiral motifs are particularly impressive. Those sites listed are Pappa Westray, Westray, Eday and Maes Howe.

One example of the continuity of use of rock-art is to be found at Cairnholy, Galloway, where a chambered-tomb with an imposing façade was excavated and found to contain an inserted cist containing a cup-and-ring marked slab (broken off something else, perhaps) and another cup-and-ring design made on the capstone (Piggott and Powell 1949). The dating of the pottery fragments and cremated bone inside the cist was not clear, however. The landscape surrounding the two impressive chambered tombs has much rock-art on outcrop, all situated within close proximity to the sea.

One other possible Neolithic site is quite different: at Lilburn (N) in the nineteenth century a pit was discovered containing not only two layers of cremations, some individual deposits capped with three small pieces of whinstone (dolerite), but also with two marked rocks alongside them. One is a broken-off slab with incomplete concentric rings without a central cup and the other, also broken, has concentric circles, a horned spiral and other curved grooves. It is not clear from the report whether anything was broken when the stones were lifted out of the pit. It is likely that what we have here is a Neolithic long barrow covering a pit burial, with the covering mound removed for field clearance, with the actual site being well visible from below and some distance around, but not at the highest part of the hill. This is another site that might repay careful excavation to confirm this thesis. The rock-art is of very high quality, as skilful as any markings on the Irish passage-graves (Beckensall 2001).

In the excavation at Dalladies, a cup-marked stone was found in a timber mortuary structure beneath a long barrow. The site had been used for a long time; the radiocarbon date given for the placing of this rock was at the end of the fourth century BC. It was partly as a result of this excavation that everyone began to consider a much earlier date for rock-art than had previously been suggested, the early reports favouring a Bronze Age date. That is now all water under the bridge, for there are examples of rock-art that has been incorporated in Early Neolithic and Early Bronze Age sites, a more extensive use than previously suspected.

Another type of burial structure found almost entirely in Scotland, but with offshoots in Northumberland is called a 'four-poster'. Four standing stones are arranged in a rough square, at the centre of which a burial may have taken place. That in Northumberland, at Goatstones has the top of one stone covered with distinct cups, whilst the others have also been found recently to have fainter cup-marks. A search around this site has also revealed many stones of varying sizes that have simple cups too, so the decoration on the four-poster is part of a wider phenomenon. The term was established by Aubrey Burl (Burl 1988), and he regards them as Early Bronze Age, though, as at Goatstones, there has been no recent excavation to demonstrate this.

In Wales there is another example: in Radnorshire, The Four Stones is a four-stone setting with three cup-marks on the upper surface of the south-western stone.

A claim that the standing stones at Balkemback (this chapter) may be a four-poster is not supported by any firm evidence, as other stones may have been removed from the site. This and other standing stones with decoration will be considered later. Stone circles are not primarily for burial, but can have burials added or have a foundation deposit of human bone. Passage-graves, cairns and other mounds are primarily for burial, but have other monumental functions too.

In a different tradition are the hundreds of cairns and barrows that are spread throughout Britain, only a few of which have rock-art incorporated in them.

CAIRNS AND ROUND BARROWS

The use of rock-art in the construction of round mounds has been found to be far greater than it was thought to be only a few years ago, thanks to research by independent and professional archaeologists.

Recently, Headland Archaeology (Internet) excavated a sub-circular kerbless cairn of c.20m diameter at Balblair, near Inverness, covering a single burial cist that had been robbed, made mostly of sandstone slabs, but with a schist capstone and end-slab. There were three decorated slabs in the cist, forming most of the stone box that had presumably contained a body with a Food Vessel and scraper, all the evidence left in the disturbed grave. Whereas the end-slab and one side-slab had one and three cups respectively, the other side-slab had a uniquely-decorated weathered face; there were two large cups, one of them perforated right through the rock. There are parallels for this in a cist slab from the Ravensheugh kerbed cairn (N) (Beckensall 2001) which had a slab with a perforation, a fallen standing stone at Ballymeanoch (K), and a cist cover from Redbrae, Dumfries (see below). However, the deeply-incised asymmetrical decoration that dominated one end of the rock differed in that it was not pecked, and was not in the cup-and-ring tradition. Instead, it belongs to the curvilinear art more usually found in passage-graves. The parallel curved lines branch from a central space. Part of the surface

ART IN BURIALS AND OTHER MONUMENTS

was broken off before the design was put on. Although the slab could have been brought in from another monument, it could also have been made specifically for this cist. We do not know for certain.

Cists were constructed to hold burials, either as cremations, inhumations or both. They are built like boxes, usually with a lid, in a pit dug into the subsoil, although the pit can be dug into upcast from the digging of a pit for an earlier burial (as at Blawearie, (N)). Some contain artefacts such as tools, pottery and jewellery. Generally they are covered with a mound of some sort, such as earth from a ditch, earth and stone, or stone. In the case of cairns, the cobbles are collected from the surface and this clearance may have had a practical value too of clearing a field for cutting hay or ploughing. The kerb, varying in size from small boulders to large standing stones, kept the material intact. At Blawearie this kerb was of large standing stones, mostly touching, some hammered for a better fit. An even more skilful kerb fitting was achieved at Chatton Sandyford (N) where the kerbs were so close that it was almost impossible to insert a blade between them – but this kerb was smaller. The Blawearie kerb surrounded a pit, which probably began as the hole left by a removed oak tree and filled in. The site then became a small cemetery, with kerbs being removed to provide cist stones, and the circle made good, in one part with a drystone wall, but all within the same historical period, the Early Bronze Age. Apart from a later insertion of a blue melon bead, dating to any period from Iron Age onward, the finds were a Food Vessel, Food Vessel Urn, amber necklace and jet and shale necklace. One cist had burnt scrapers accompanying the cremation burials.

When Ronald Morris catalogued rock-art sites in southern Scotland (Morris 1981) he included all the decorated slabs in cists. Compared with the number of open-air sites and graves, there are very few. What is clear is that many were found from the early nineteenth century onwards, that some of them subsequently disappeared, and others ended up in museums; the reported rock-art shows that the slabs were on the whole broken off already-decorated outcrop, for the motifs are often cut through. Another observation is that the motifs represented in cists are not the usual cup-and-ring types, but include concentric rings without a central cup, concentric arcs, and meandering grooves. Almost all that are in a datable context are associated with Late Neolithic/Early Bronze Age finds, mainly Beakers, Food Vessels, and Food Vessel Urns. This gives the burial itself a rough date, but the incorporated slabs could be much earlier. The Balblair cairn is not alone.

Compared with the way we deal with almost destroyed sites today, when we still find residual evidence of use and timescale, these early reports can be very vague, but are all we have to go on. However, taking all the design elements together, there is a picture of what went into cist construction. Ronald Morris divided southern Scotland into zones for his study (Morris 1981b): westward through Dumfries and Galloway, northwards from the Borders of Cumbria and Northumberland through Ayr to the Glasgow region, the Lothians around Edinburgh, Fife, Central Scotland, Arran and Argyll. Argyll and Galloway were not treated in such detail as the others because he had already written books about them. Other zones listed are Orkney, the Hebrides, and Highland.

As the finding of decorated cist slabs is so widely scattered and so dependent on chance, or because of the interest of some local antiquarian, the distribution may not give the real picture. However, we have to go on what we have. It is rare to have a recently-excavated site like Balblair or Balbirnie. Some of the stones of the reported excavations are safely housed in museums, so at least the motifs can be studied and accurately recorded. What follows is an overview of these decorated cist slabs.

Only one has been noted in Galloway in a definite context: at Cairn Holy. In Dumfries, a cist cover found at Redbrae (C) near Wigtown, first reported in 1947, was a roughly-hexagonal Greywacke slab carved on both sides, the outward-facing having six cups and three incised grooves, and the other five cups and 16 grooves and scratches, with a very faint pattern of three diamonds. A hole goes completely through the centre of the stone, and this may be compared with Balblair and Ravensheugh (above).

At Kirkdale House, Galloway, there is a collection of slabs found as a result of trenching waste ground, and reported by Sir James Simpson in 1864. Although it is impossible to give it a context, the High Auchenlarie slab, is a possible cist slab; its remarkable range of motifs in any case makes it one of the most important decorated stones in Britain (illustration on p.40).

The Ayr region has four examples. Beoch has a dolerite slab on the floor of the cist with sets of concentric rings and arcs, clearly pecked, but broken off a larger slab. Beaker pottery fragments and cinerary urns were found when it was first reported in 1937.

The Border region has produced only one, at Drumelzier, a possible cist cover that came from near a mound where a cist cover was missing. Reported by J.H. Craw in 1929, associated with a Beaker, Urns and part of a jet armlet, it has four groups of two concentric circles, and a single circle, all without central cups and all with shallow incisions rather than pecking.

The Royal National Museum of Scotland has examples of decorated cist slabs on display, along with a collection of associated finds and splendid examples of carvings of a later period.

The La Mancha slab, a flat broken red sandstone, was 'found in a gravel bank', first reported by Sir James Simpson. Its original site on the farm is unknown.

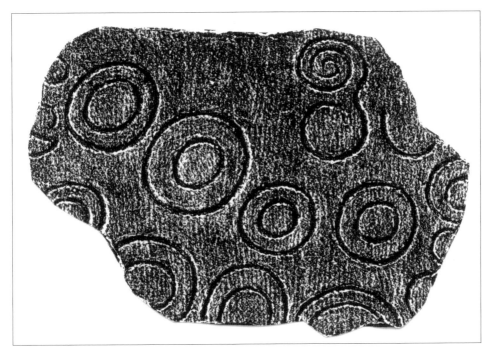

78 La Mancha. *Sir James Simpson*

At Wester Yardhouses a gritstone cover first reported in 1872 from a cairn associated with Beaker pottery, has a partly broken-off surface, but the remaining decoration is most unusual as it includes zoned triangles. There are also concentric rings and arcs without a central cup. As if to emphasise this tradition, a short stone cist with a slab marked on the inner side of its lid, now missing, had similar concentric circles and arcs.

The Letham Grange stone (Angus), decorated on two sides, is thought originally to have come from a cist, later to be incorporated in a souterrain. The photograph, taken of it in the museum, was part of a research project, and shows clearly the pristine pick-marks and the way in which the whole of the surface was decorated.

The Coilsfield cist cover is now missing. First reported by J. Patterson in 1852, it was sketched by Sir James Simpson (Plate XIII), who reported that in 1785 General Montgomery sent a drawing of it to the Royal Society at Edinburgh, so he had to copy the 'rough original drawing of it' for publication. It had once 'covered an urn'. It is interesting, as the dominant motif is concentric rings around a cup, from which a groove runs, with mini cups inside the outer ring and the fifth arranged concentric to them, rather like those on outcrop in Galloway. There are also spiral-type and serpentine motifs, and concentric arcs and rings.

Above: 79 Wester
Yardhouses cist slab
(1m long). *Royal
Museums of Scotland.*

Left: 80 Letham
Grange stone

The Glasgow region has a well-known stone from *Knappers*: a gritstone cist-cover now in Kelvingrove Museum, reported by J.M. Davidson in 1934, found with bones, flint, pottery, bronze and lignite. In the cist itself was a polished-flint axe. The emphasis here is again on pecked circular motifs, three with two concentric rings, with no cups at the centre. In the Lothians region, at Caerlowrie a short stone cist with marks on the inner side of its lid, now missing, was sketched from an old sketch (Simpson 1864), and is covered with cups-and-rings.

At *Graigie Hill* a cist cover, now safely housed in the National Museum, was drawn by Simpson (XV) with sketches that illustrate where it was found in *c.*1824 (illustration 6.68).

At Ferniegair among a number of cists found in a sand deposit, one had a side-slab marked on two faces – very unusual in Britain as a whole. It was weathered and broken off a larger slab. Its context was with a burial with a Food Vessel, Beaker, and flint artefacts in the same cemetery.

The fact that so many of these slabs have been broken off outcrops suggests not just the use of that rock as building material, but its selection as something appropriate for a cist burial, with a significance known only to the builders.

At Parkburn a cist stone now in the Museum of Antiquities, Edinburgh, has arcs. Only one decorated cist stone comes from the Central Region, from Tillicoultry House Ground, where a cist slab at the centre of a stone circle was reported as having its sides and upper surface decorated (R. Robertson in 1894). By 1898 it had already become so eroded that not only were the figures shallow, but some had completely disappeared. With it was a Food Vessel and cremated bone. A site listed in Morris's 1989 survey is a cist with rings at Kings Meadows.

Finally, in Fife there is the now well-publicised discovery at Balbirnie, a site excavated recently (Richie 1974, Burl 1979), when five cists were uncovered from cairns within a ring of stones, including one that had cups-and-rings inside facing inwards on a side-slab. Another cist had 16 cups, mostly in lines. The associations are with flint knife, Beaker, Food Vessels, cinerary urn sherds and jet. Replicas have been placed on site, with the originals transferred to the National Museum of Antiquities.

Further north, Ronald Morris has listed cist sites with decoration. He notes lines on a cist at Brodgar and lozenges on a cist in the Hebrides, at Kilchattan. In the Highland Region his listing includes these sites: Carn Laith tomb, with a ring, Embo Street cist with a 'spade', a now-untraceable rectangle on a cist slab from Ardross, a spiral on a cist at Catterline, this stone being now at the Aberdeen University Anthropological Museum, and a cup-and-ring mark on a cist at Ardmarnoch, Cowal.

One interesting example of how rock-art can be taken from an outcrop and the rock 're-sanctified' is at North Plantation, Fowberry (N). Here, an

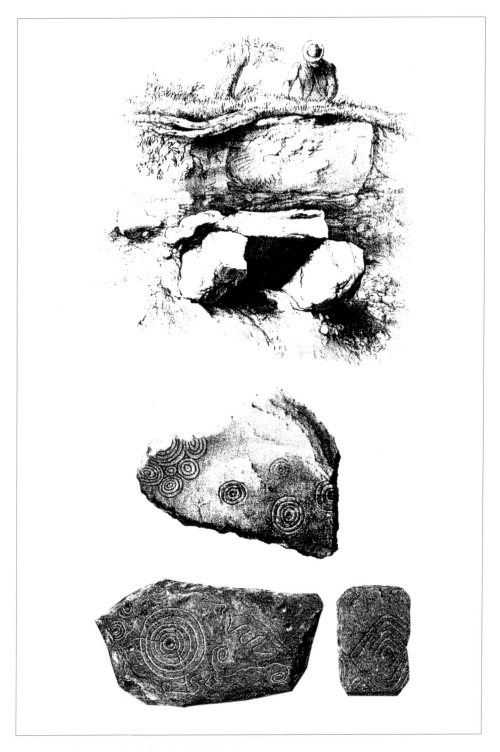

81 Cragie Hill (top and middle), Coilsfield, Badden

82 Balbirnie cist, Morris archive. *Crown Copyright: RCAHMS*

83 North plantation, Fowberry (N)

undisturbed outcrop incorporated into an Iron Age enclosure has had a rectangular slab removed from a surface that is covered with eroded motifs of the cup-and-ring type, and a similar motif pecked onto the lower surface from which the slab has been removed. We may assume that one use of this removed slab in prehistory was to form the cover of a cist, as there are many destroyed burial cairns in the same area. When I first uncovered the rock, it occurred to me that the reason the lower motif had survived in such a pristine condition was that it had been covered, perhaps by natural vegetation, very quickly after its re-marking, whereas the rest had been open to the elements. This is always an important consideration when we ask how far a rock surface has been eroded, as it depends on how long it was exposed. Many cairns and mounds contain cist burials, some of them with decorated stones, some of which are unweathered and purpose-made, and others broken off an outcrop that may already have decoration on it, sometimes eroded, so this site may be the source of such use. Cists were not the only ways of interring the dead: some burials may be in pits with a single small capstone, and some of these too may have a cup-mark. The body may even have been laid out at ground level with a heap of stones over it. The problem of trying to work out a timescale for erosion is difficult. Not only does it depend on weather conditions, but also on the type of rock (hard, soft), on whether it was covered over for part or all of its life. Differential weathering (i.e. unevenly over a surface) may account for some motifs being fainter than others even though they were pecked on the rock at the same time. Another factor is that some motifs may have been pecked lightly at the outset, and others deeper. There are many examples of outcrop surfaces in Northumberland where slabs have been removed and new marks added to the surfaces from which the rock has been removed, all in the same general tradition.

Cairns, then, may have cists that incorporate rock-art, but some have markings on their kerbstones. Kerbs are a logical device for retaining the cobbles on a mound; they also define the mound more clearly as a special place, another stone circle. Sometimes the markings face outwards, and others face inwards. Sometimes there is more than one kerb, concentric to it. It is not always easy to distinguish a clearance-cairn from a burial without excavation, but in clusters on the edge of field systems they are likely to be the former.

Another device to incorporate rock-art into a mound is to collect cobble stones from the surrounding area, mark them with cups and cups-and-rings, or linear grooves, sometimes on more than one surface, then include them in the cairn material. Whether this is true or not, it does seem to be reminiscent of the way in which people today bring wreaths to a funeral. Where sites have been excavated using modern methods, even though the original mound may have been partially destroyed, as at Weetwood (N), many of these cobbles were found to be deposited face-down, and others are covered over by other cobbles. Although kerbs marked on their outer faces can be seen, those inside the mound cannot, and were not intended to be. This also applies to inward-facing kerbs such as those at Weetwood, Fowberry (N) and Fylingdales (NYM). The same applies, as we have seen, to some art in Irish passage-graves, although the latter could be re-entered/re-accessed for ceremonies of reburial, or for some other reason not quite clear to us. Cairns were usually a one-off monument and sealed at the time of their construction. Any additions were made by removing a small part of the mound and inserting a new burial, as at Blawearie (N). This superficial use extended in the case of Money Mound in Sussex into the Iron Age/Roman period with the burial of many votive offerings. A cairn at Chatton Sandyford (N) and the one at Blawearie (N) have Iron Age/Roman material buried in them too.

In the area around these sites are earthfast blocks and boulders, lying among cairns that are decorated with cups and cups-and-rings. The same feature is also found on the Otterburn ranges at the Bellshield Law cairnfield, where, within close reach of one of the rare Northumberland long cairns, are three decorated embedded boulders

The Blawearie and Chatton Sandyford cairns mounds were meticulously excavated recently, and so was the important site at Fulforth Farm, Witton Gilbert, near Durham city. This had no covering mound, but, like Chatton Sandyford, had some rock-art in a datable context. A cist was exposed when the cover was dragged away during ploughing, later to be completely excavated, including a large area around it. This proved particularly profitable, as another, boat-shaped pit packed with cobbles and interspersed cremations had a plano-convex knife along its axis at the base. The decorated rocks are crucial to our understanding of how they were used. The cist cover was not reused, eroded outcrop but a completely decorated purpose-cut slab with cups-and-rings facing into the cist. The top of this cover was covered with a simpler decoration of cups and linked cups, plough-scratched from above. Inside the cist were two decorated rocks, one of which acted as a prop for the cover, with the decoration showing pristine peck-marking. The cover did not cover the whole of the cist, for one exposed end was packed with cobbles and cremations, with a corner marked by a re-ground polished stone axe, blade uppermost. Although the decoration of the cist cover was cups and cups-and-rings, the inserted blocks included parallel serpentine grooves and two cups with single rings. There is no reason to suppose that all were made at different periods (Beckensall and Laurie 1998).

The discovery of other large slabs of elaborately-decorated stone has not been made in undisturbed graves like this in County Durham, but one found at Gainsford, now in the Bowes Museum, Barnard Castle, has a complex design of grooves zoning the rock, separating groups of concentric rings around cups, but

84 Fulforth farm decorated stone supporting the cist cover (D), 36cm long

the obverse side has simple cups linked by grooves. This has much in common with the Fulforth Farm slab. Another slab outside the Bowes Museum from Greta Bridge, reused as the cover of a Roman grave, has a scatter of well-defined cups, curved connected grooves and three curved chevrons – an unusual motif.

In the Kilmartin area three cist slabs still lie among the ruins of burial mounds destroyed by quarrying, all with simple cup-marks, at Poltalloch.

In the same area, there is a cist slab in an excavated and restored cairn at Nether Largie which is covered with cup-marks, here overlaid by pecked representations of metal axes. Many of the Kilmartin cairns have a few cups in their structures, including some inside cists.

Another surviving cist cover is exposed at Carn Ban, with a cup and lines on its top surface. (Note that *Carn Ban* is a different site from the outcrop site Cairnbaan, although in the same general area.)

Cumbrian mounds of different periods have incorporated decorated stones. The Old Parks site has a spine of five large stones, three of which are decorated, although this is in the form of unfurling fronds ('walking sticks') and small enclosures possibly belonging to the site when it was a Neolithic long barrow, later to be reused for Early Bronze Age cremations, then destroyed by quarrying for road stone. Two later structures are to be found at Moor Divock ring-cairn and at Hardendale Circle Cairn In the former, there is a cup-and-ring on a large

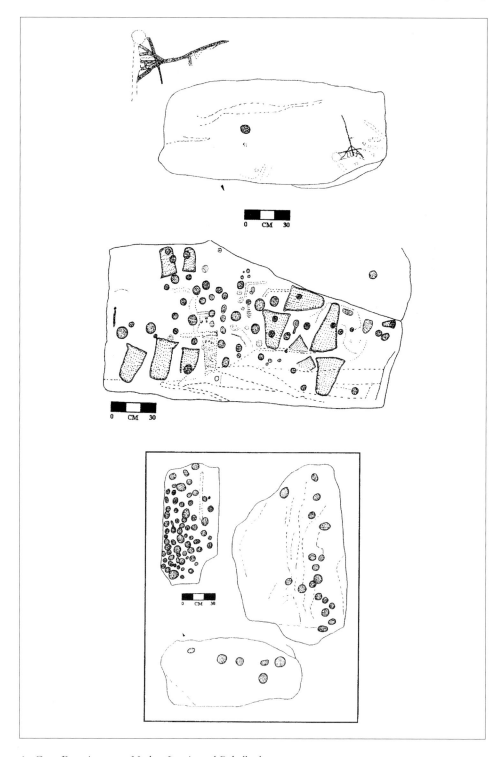

85 Carn Ban cist cover, Nether Largie and Poltalloch

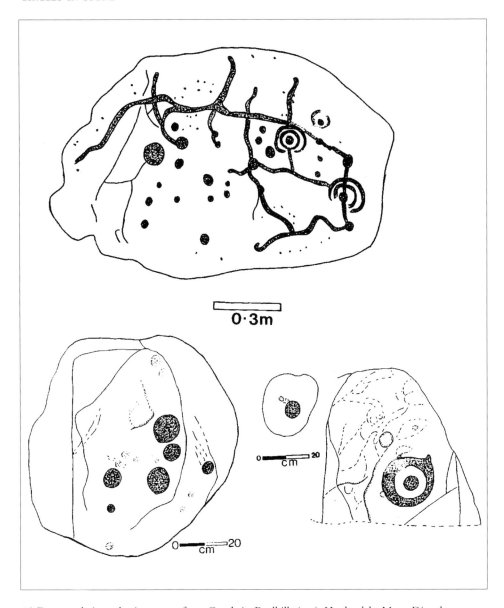

86 Decorated cist and cairn stones from Cumbria: Redhills (top), Hardendale, Moor Divock

kerbstone and a loose cup-marked cobble at the destroyed centre, where there had been a pit with ashes and pottery sherds and above it a broken Food Vessel. The Hardendale cairn has large cup-marks on a sandstone boulder in the kerb. One site, Redhills, now destroyed, along with the decorated cist cover reported from it with a drawing, showed a slab with long linear grooves, cups and cups-and-rings (Beckensall 2002).

Sometimes the cup-marked stones protrude from the vegetation on cairns to indicate possible associations with burials, only to be proved by excavation. Barningham Moor has six of these, notably in the area of How Tallon, a large round barrow with multiple burials, pottery and flints of the Early Bronze Age, and at least eight cup-marked cobbles unrecorded at the time of the dig in 1897, that still remain in the wall built over the cairn. A low-profile cairn with three marked stones sticking out of it at Frankinshaw How is unexplored, and so is a cairn above the head of Osmonds Gill with cups, linear and curved grooves on a large stone protruding from it.

In Wensleydale there is a particularly prominent cairn at Addlebrough on a summit, turf covered, with four large, marked slabs visible on the surface (Beckensall and Laurie 1998).

Very few burials in North-West Yorkshire have marked rocks incorporated, yet the North Yorkshire Moors area has many, most of which have been drawn together by Brown and Chappell.

As the synthesis of data about the North Yorkshire Moors has been a recent and thorough task (Brown and Chappell 2005), it is useful to look at what has been revealed here, then widen the field to include other British examples. There has been a tendency to rely too much on a few over-worked examples. Most of those here come from excavations that were not conducted according to modern standards. There was a great interest in contents of burials in the nineteenth century, and hundreds were dug. Modern farming has removed many of these as well as others, so the task of discovering what was found in them is difficult. However, some general observations and specific examples given by Brown and Chappell are revealing.

The south-west of the region shows that all the marked rocks there have come from burial sites excavated/dug in the past 150 years, along the fertile slopes of the southern fringe of the moor. These include simple cups. In one case, a disturbed cairn on Ireton Moor 5, excavated in 1973, was constructed of two concentric kerb circles with a central setting of boulders. Many excavated cairns demonstrate that hidden beneath mounds, concentric arrangements of stones occur. A cup-marked stone was found among cremated bone, a plano-convex knife, sherds of a Bronze Age pot and Food Vessel Urn, all indicating a date around 4000 years ago. However, the cairn had been built on a site already used in Neolithic times, for there was a deep pit surrounded by two ditches, a pot, cremated bone, and a leaf-shaped arrowhead. This is another example of the continuous use of a special site over hundreds of years. In other areas decorated outcrop may form the base of the cairn (as at Fowberry and Lordenshaw (N)). When it is on outcrop, it may be impossible to determine how long one use and another followed each other, whereas it is clearly demonstrated at Ireton Moor.

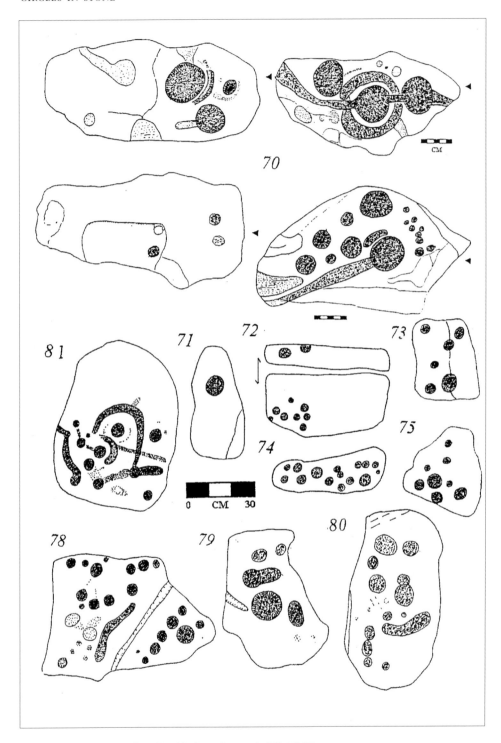

87 Cairn stones: How Tallon, Frankinshaw, Osmonds Gill (all D)

88 Addlebrough decorated cairn stone in a wider setting

In the same area, at Ireton Moor 6, a mound, again excavated in 1973, revealed that it was constructed of three concentric kerbs with a cupmarked stone in the outer kerb. The grave had been robbed, but Food Vessel sherds and worked flints remained. The Way Hagg barrow was excavated by Tissiman in 1848, in which there were three cup-marked stones near an accessory ('incense'/'pigmy') cup and large collared urn. There were 25 other cup-marked stones, including one with parallel grooves on its edge.

A 1965 excavation of a plough-damaged mound at Hutton Buscel exposed a kerbed barrow with an inner ring of stones built over a limestone paving, covering an inhumation, Food Vessel, and Beaker sherds, a small stone-lined pit with charcoal and hazelnut shells. In its last phase of construction, a kerb of 60 stones was laid around it, nine with cups, one with incised lines and cups and one with drilled holes. One of these stones had a characteristic local 'comb' pattern.

When one considers the extent of barrow digging in the area, finds such as these are very much a minority. James Ruddock himself opened 90 barrows in the Pickering area in the mid-nineteenth century.

Bearing in mind the rapidity with which digging took place and the extent of it, it is more than likely that marked stones would have been overlooked unless they were spectacular decorated slabs.

In the southern area of the Moors there are no examples of open-air rock-art, probably because the soft limestone was unsuitable. If the burials contain rock-art, sandstones are used. At Byland Moor, among many of the barrows excavated by Canon Greenwell, one cairn had 20 marked stones, some with up to six cups and others with cups connected by grooves. At Lingmoor Barrow, Hutton-le-Hole, a 1969-70 excavation of a mound covering a single kerb of stones around a central cairn with three cremation pots, single cups were found on two kerbstones. Additionally, two stones near the cremation had a pecked surface with a single cup, and part of a saddle quern that lay alongside the barrow had a cup-mark.

In the western sites listed by Brown and Chappell, formed by the Hambleton and Cleveland Hills, where limestone gives way to sandstone, rock-art appears on exposed surfaces. At Thimbleby the authors located a fine cup-and-ring boulder which they think may have been displaced from a burial, and many small cup-marked stones associated with cairns, some having cups on two sides and some built into nearby walls.

Sites in the Eston Hills, northern sites and the Cleveland coast have revealed a considerable number of decorated rocks associated with burial. At Ords Barrow 2, one of many excavated in the nineteenth century, one marked stone covered a cremation in a large collared urn, with intersecting linear grooves on the underside. The northern sites include Kemplah Top cairn, Guisborough, where a kerbed-cairn covered a cist cover with three cups, an inside slab with one, covering a Handled Beaker.

The Cleveland coast has been most productive. The Hinderwell Beacon is a classic, because over 300 marked rocks were recovered from the mound during several years of excavation. The mound covered an internal wall of c.9m diameter, circles within circles again, which enclosed seven cremations with Food Vessels (Hornsby and Laverick 1920). Roughly half the stones were cup-marked, others were marked with incised lines, and several had been partly ground or polished. This use of so many marked stones in a mound links well with sites in Northumberland and County Durham.

Four barrows at Boulby include marked stones associated with an interment, a flint, a cremation, a shale pendant, an inverted Collared Urn and a Food Vessel. Among the important recent excavations, conducted by Blaise Vyner, is The Street House Cairn, Loftus and The Street House Wossit, interpreted as a palisaded ritual enclosure. Both these sites are fully documented, and it needs only a brief comment on the place of rock-art there. The Cairn was a kerbed round barrow, part of a sequence beginning with a Neolithic long barrow built over a wooden mortuary structure. Several stones that were cup-marked were thought to be from the Neolithic cairn, then used in the northern kerb of the later cairn. On this site the time span is from c.3200 BC to 1900 BC, during which long period the rocks could have been marked and used.

The Wossit, unique as a monument (thus the name), with its spaced circles of timber posts around a central pit with two uprights, was originally constructed c.2200 BC, and when the timbers were removed and their trenches and the central pit back-filled, a stone capping containing 12 marked stones was added, and their addition was associated with cremations in a Collared urn, Grooved Ware, a Beaker, jet, flint and two saddle querns. This capping sealed in the destroyed earlier site, and it is likely that the cup-marked stones were therefore made or used for that purpose.

The purpose of mounds was both to cover and draw attention to burials. They are not necessarily sites at the highest place in the landscape, but are usually visible from afar. What proportion of the population had such treatment we do not know as although there must have been thousands of these mounds all over Britain, it is likely that others did not go out in such style, perhaps even being left to rot. Normally the mounds are of the Late Neolithic/Early Bronze Age period, although they are sometimes built over earlier ones, as we have seen. Sometimes a stone circle may be reused for burial, as at Temple Wood (Kilmartin) or Long Meg (C). Standing Stone Rigg (NY) has as its focus an elaborately decorated cist.

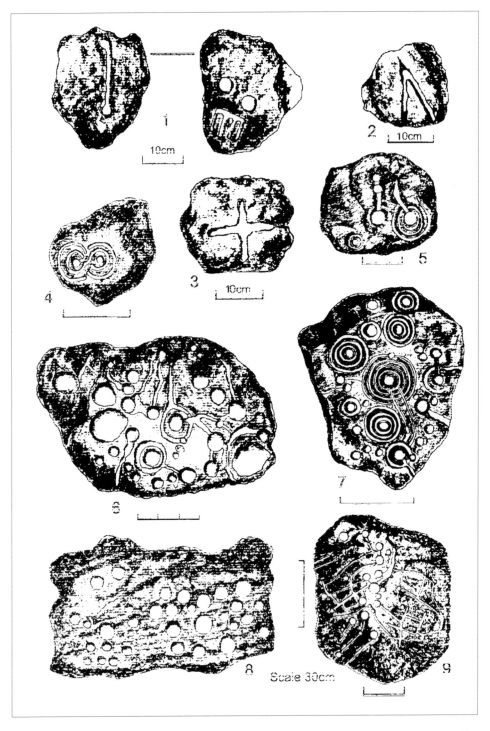

89 Top: Hinderwell Beacon and other cairn stones. Middle: Standing Stone Rigg 7 and Eston Nabb hillfort (NYM). *Paul Brown*

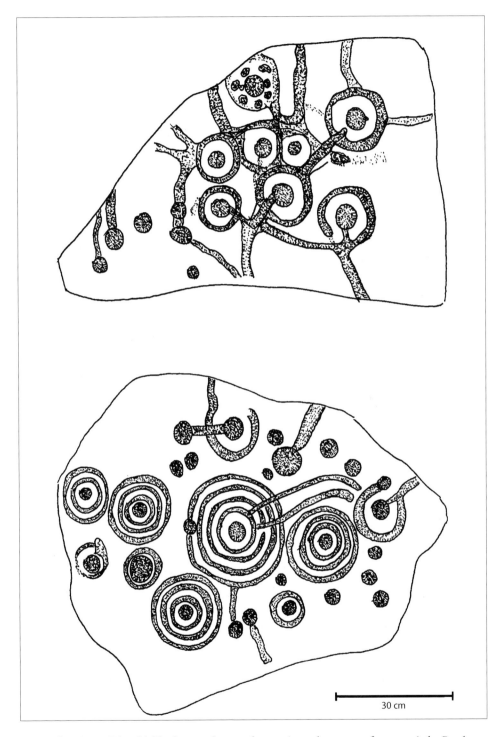

30 cm

90 Standing Stone Rigg: highly decorated stones from a cist at the centre of a stone circle. *Based on Paul Brown's drawings*

In all these cases a place of special importance continued to be used centuries later. This happens too in a few cases in Northumberland where mounds are built over outcrop rock that has been decorated. The Fowberry cairn is a classic example of a double-kerbed mound with four of its kerbs marked (three facing inwards) and over 20 of its cobble stones marked, being built on a stretch of *c.* 20m of lavishly-decorated outcrop, some of it lost as a result of recent quarrying. There was no organic layer between outcrop and mound, so presumably the cairn had been built onto the newly-decorated surface immediately. At Lordenshaw a mound was similarly built on cup-marked outcrop, with one of its kerbstones having cups on its outward face. In the same area the 'Horseshoe Rock' may be the kerb of a barrow, in this case profusely decorated. North across the River Coquet from these sites is another large cairn, known as Football Cairn, with massive disturbed cists, built on outcrop that has cups-and-rings. In all these cases the rock-art on cairns does not stand in isolation, for these are some of the richest areas of landscape rock-art in the country.

At Dod Law, many miles to the north-east, another decorated outcrop has the remains of a cairn upon it, while in the same area, at The Ringes: a fine large panel of outcrop art, there is a possibly earthen mound built over it. There is much potential for investigating similar occurrences. At Weetwood there is another largely unexplored cairn, disturbed at its centre, built on and into decorated outcrop rock (Beckensall 2001b).

One such potential site has been recently excavated at Hunterheugh Crag (NU 1175 1678) (Waddington 2005) and promises much information. I found and recorded this site, working on a discovery by Tim Gates during his survey along the line of a gas pipeline which ran close to it. He found a patch of outcrop with very well-defined cups-and-rings, mostly pristine, north of the site that I later found. His site had a scatter of small cobbles. The excavated site was a large outcrop that formed the edge of a small scarp east of a Romano-British settlement that had thrown up many stone-walled enclosures. The discrete outcrop had a thin scatter of cobbles, but in between there were cups and cups-and-rings visible. One particular group was a sophisticated pattern, and one of its serpentine grooves disappeared under some of these cobbles. Believing this to be a possible cairn, I did not disturb it, pending proper excavation. Along the ridge were other marked rocks, part of the same outcrop, and some later appeared within the enclosure and to the north-west on another outcrop. Previously all this was, of course, unknown, except for a mention in the Northumberland County History that there were some cups in the area regarded as being natural.

There is a cautionary tale here for those who may expect excavation to solve many problems, for it sometimes happens that excavation may raise even more

91 Hunterheugh excavation site (N) with a Romano-British settlement in the background

questions than it answers. The excavation discovered a little more rock-art, some of it faint and some deep. The outcrop in places had been prised apart with wedges, and the excavator thought that one gap thus formed may have been used as a grave. This however was inconclusive: nothing was found in the gap to justify this and certainly no artefacts or datable material, so it remains only a possibility. The rock-art was considered to be phased, but it is difficult to understand how when there was no soil stratigraphy or finds to support it. There was a statement that the rock had been quarried and later motifs added to the newly-exposed surface, suggesting by the erosion of one surface compared with another to be a 'considerable' time gap. It is thought that two large pieces of quarried rock with these early markings had been moved to the centre of the outcrop and 'a cist constructed between these two quarried slabs with three sandstone blocks set on their edges to form the sides of a box and at the base of the box the rock had been quarried down to create a deeper void', with the cairn piled over the top. It is also suggested that a secondary insertion was made, a stone setting 'towards the top of the cairn which may have served as a grave'. The whole site had become the focus for a long wall that ran from the enclosure, during which time the search for stone to build walls for that and many other animal enclosures dotted around the area must have caused

92 Beanley slab (N), newly-discovered and likely to provide much information from its context (scale: 50cm)

some disturbance to many outcrops. One good reason to support the idea that the cairn was constructed for burial is that five of the stones of the cairn were lightly decorated and this links them to other cairn sites where this occurs.

The moorland of Beanley, where these finds were made, and this site explored, has potential for further exploration. Already we have found more landscape art, but the greatest potential site that I discovered is a superb panel of rock in an area from which other supposed cist slabs have been removed (one particularly fine one to Alnwick Castle Museum). My recent find was jutting out from grass inside an oval stone-dump wall enclosure; the only exposed part, covered with only thin grass, is pictured above, and may be part of a larger structure of flat slabs.

I have suggested to local University departments that the excavation of this site gives an opportunity not only of revealing the rest of this exceptional design, but of examining its context. It is not often that rock-art is set in a small oval enclosure.

County Durham, Swaledale and Wensleydale have similar potential for further investigation, as we already know from cairns with visible rock-art incorporated, as well as those from which it has been removed.

The Peak District is the most southerly district where English rock-art appears in any density. From 48 decorated rocks in 1982, this number has risen to 67 in 2003, found on sandstones and gritstones, but not on limestone. There are some regional characteristics in perhaps 25 of the 67 rocks in a repertoire that varies from complex to simple motifs and symbols. Most of the marked rocks are portables, largely found in burials. Eight are within barrows, three in smaller cairns and one embedded in the kerb of a stone circle. Stanage Barrow has a stone with motifs on three faces, some linked with a groove, six on the upper surface, eight on the west side and four on south. Another slab on the disturbed surface has been broken, but when the two pieces are joined they show that the cups are joined by grooves in a zigzag.

The Barbrook Barrow has a cup with a shallow ring. A small cairn at Gardom's Edge has a single cup on a pecked, flat surface, and a similar stone comes from Ball Cross. During restoration in 1989, two portable gritstones with single cups were found inside and outside the disturbed fabric of the bank of the Barbrook II stone circle, to add to six listed earlier.

Barnatt's comments that 'several carvings from monuments appear unworn' suggests that they were fresh at the time of the creation of the monument, and thus made for it. The Peak barrows have on the whole only isolated examples of decorated stones, mostly cups, but the important thing is that people are aware and looking for them.

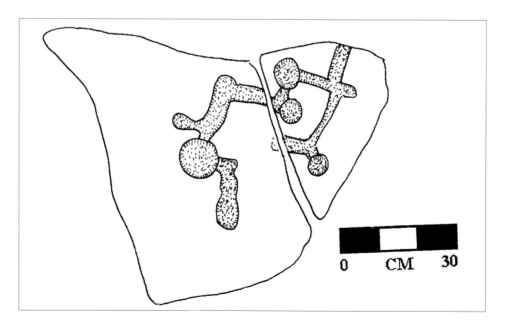

93 Stanage (P) broken cist stone

A recent article (Guilbert, Garlton and Walters 2006) has reported a decorated gritstone boulder within a detailed landscape survey. Among the round barrows in Wales, The Crick Barrow (Savory 1940) has two blocks of sandstone with 23 and 17 cups forming part of the kerb in two quadrants.

It is not clear why the south of England and South-West have so little rock-art, apart, of course, from not having the outcrop surfaces suitable for it, but there is some in burials. Fourteen locations of marked rocks in Cornwall are in monuments. I have already listed these in *British Prehistoric Rock Art* (Beckensall 1999, 2002 pp.83-5). Other sites also listed are in Dorset and Somerset (pp.86-7). Since then, John Coles has looked again at the site of the Pool Farm cist cover and established a date for the burial, about 4000 years ago. Among recent finds, a decorated stone from Knowlton (Lewis *et al.* 2000) a small boulder with cups may have come from a nearby round barrow. At Chivelstone, Devon, (Waterhouse 2000) a stone marked on both sides with cups on both surfaces may have come from a barrow.

On Fylingdales Moor (NYM) a recent discovery of a cairn with spectacular rock-art incorporated into the kerb and including small decorated stones was made by Paul Frodsham when he visited the fire-ravaged area with Graham Lee and Robert White, National Park archaeologists. When Paul Brown and Graeme Chappell visited the site in April 2004 they saw that the large, flat slab had been revealed by 0.5m (Brown and Chappell 2005), with much of its triangular patterning visible, regrettably exposed by a member of the public. Some root matting had blown away to leave an exposed section of another kerb top, this time rounded. All this was reported to English Heritage who fortunately appointed Blaise Vyner to excavate the site, but the excavation was restricted to the kerb where the stone was visible.

The location of the site is restricted, so no grid reference will be given here, but it is worth noting that within 24 hours of the discovery the site location and pictures were emailed to Graeme Chappell by 'bloggers', who were asked not to spread the word further.

The stone proved to be part of a kerb, including marked and unmarked stones. The area had many prominent cairns, made more visible by the burning of heather, and the same fire exposed a whole prehistoric surface where enclosures, stone heaps, decorated boulders and flints of many periods were to be found. This gave a great opportunity for research, as most of it was normally under thick heather.

Because this site has added much to our thoughts about rock-art, I shall make some observations, beginning with the large panel, which I wrote at the time and forwarded to colleagues on the English Heritage RAMASES committee.

GENERAL DESCRIPTION

In general, this appears to be an ice-smoothed slab, used as a kerbstone of a ring-cairn with the decoration facing inwards. Apart from the edges, there are no signs of damage or erosion. Any peripheral wear could be the result of its having been carried to the site and levered into position. Every pick-mark is clear. The edges are fairly uniform, and pose a question of whether the slab was decorated on outcrop, then broken off, or whether it was lifted as a slab dumped by ice, then decorated. The decoration is not in the cup-and-ring tradition, as it is predominantly based on straight lines, resembling pottery decoration in a Late Neolithic/Early Bronze Age tradition.

DETAILED DESCRIPTION

For convenience, I have divided the rock into zones, all having some similarities and some differences. The diagram shows these as six, labelled A as the main central panel, subdivided into 4; then B–F from left to right.

Section A
This lies at the heart of the decoration: a rectangle which is divided into four other rectangles, each with variations on the straight-line theme.

In this narrow horizontal band there is a line of four linked, complete lozenge-shapes, each with a central punched hollow, and at the edges the design continues only minimally before reaching the vertical sides of the box.

Above (1), a grid pattern of lozenge-shapes, all connected, some lines straight and others slightly curved, fills most of the box, with the exception of the far right. At the top is a line of punched small hollows.

Below (1) and (2), this rectangle has two main lines crossing from the corners, forming a saltire cross. Above its centre are two chevrons parallel to the oblique lines. Below is only one chevron; whether some small peck-marks in the remaining space may herald the start of a second is not known. To the right and left the spaces are filled with horizontal lines running from the box edges to the central crossed lines. There are 12 on the left and 13 on the right, but the main impression is one of symmetrical hatching.

(4) To the left of these three subdivisions is a narrow, vertically-placed rectangle, bounded by a row of small punched hollows, framing the rectangle on three sides, but not to the right. The top row of hollows continues into (2). There is a vertical row of lozenges to the left with extended grooves to the right, roughly forming triangles. One of the latter has three parallel grooves drawn across to

join A (3)'s pattern. Near the top, a lozenge has two interior grooves. Below is a slightly curved groove that links to the pattern of the next rectangle.

Section B
This is a vertical rectangle containing linked lozenge-shapes which end near the bottom of the slab.

Section C
The left edge of the slab has roughly V-shaped grooves that fit into the rectangle, truncated at the top, an extension of the pattern in B, slotting into the Vs. Whether these have been added to keep the pattern moving to the edge, or have been truncated by breakage, is difficult to say.

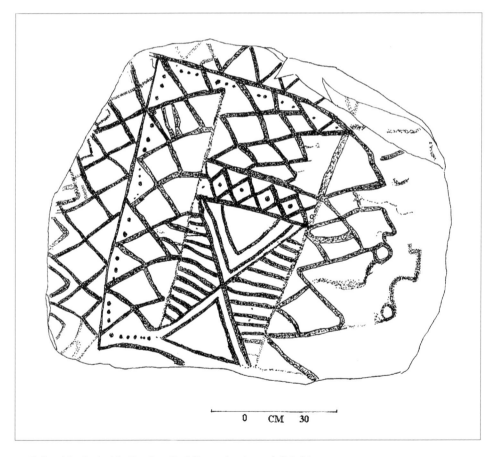

94 Fylingdales kerb slab. *Based on Paul Brown drawing and digital images*

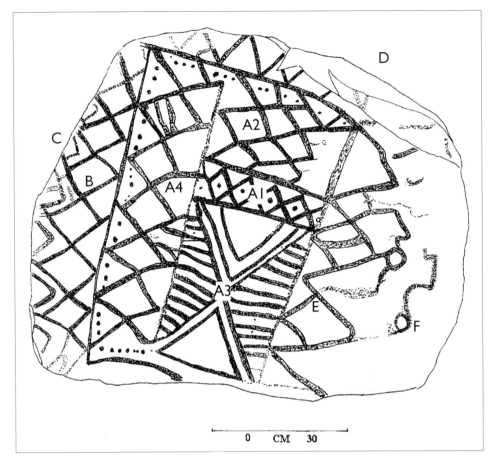

95 Fylingdales kerb: zones

Section D
The top edge of Section D has some triangles with their points to the edge, mostly clearly defined, but towards the right they are not so clear. There is some (recent?) damage at the top of the slab.

Section E
On this section, joining the right hand edge of A's rectangle, is a deeply-pecked serpentine groove which forms three triangular points, facing right. The top one meets the corner of rectangle A, touches on the top line of (1), and touches again on two of the termini of the horizontal hatching. A final line follows the general direction to reach the bottom of the slab. The second and third triangles formed by this serpentine groove have additional marking, the upper forming a lozenge inside, and the lower one a fainter lozenge with peck marks inside.

Section F

F is linked with E in that one lozenge within the serpentine groove is extended faintly to the only circle on the slab by a line and a serpentine groove. To the right is another serpentine grove, rather like a random squiggle, drawn down the rock. There are other tentative pick-marks, and some areas are left blank. It appears that this part of the slab does not continue the mainstream decoration, and could be an addition, but still with tenuous links with the main design.

My overall view of this is:
1. There is a dominant idea running through the patterns, with some minor variations on the themes, and a very interesting organisation of the whole surface into rectangles within rectangles. This makes the art form quite sophisticated, and points to considerable thought, attention to detail, and to a desire for variation. There is a general impact of the overall effect, and a pressure on us to examine each part of the pattern in detail.
2. There is nothing quite like it in British rock-art, even though some of the motifs may be familiar.

The closest parallel to the pattern is at Kilmartin (Beckensall 2005), on the Badden cist end-slab, facing inwards (NR 858 890). The slab, in Glasgow Art Gallery and Museum, made of Ardrishaig phyllite, has a multiple lozenge decoration that is cut through at either end to take the side-slabs of the cist – a characteristic of cist construction in that part of Argyll. My new survey, more detailed, includes comments in an article by Marion Campbell, J.G. Scott and Stuart Piggott that we might look to Central Europe for parallels, as some cists in the Saale valley have side-slabs decorated with 'pecked, incised or painted geometrical designs (mainly zigzags, chevrons, lozenges and similar motifs)'. They speculated on whether this type of decoration may be a 'representation of patterned textile hangings' (Campbell, Scott and Piggott 1960). The important point is that these examples are incorporated in burial structures, not by any means in a widespread, general way, but as a great rarity.

Another parallel is the rock-art of the passage-graves of Ireland.
3. I have often wondered why the designs on prehistoric pottery are so rarely echoed in rock-art, yet here we have a clear parallel with pottery design, especially Beaker pottery.
4. Other questions can be answered only by those who have excavated the site and will, hopefully, complete its assessment. We need associations. We need to know for whom the mound was built, and when. Already other panels of rock-art have been found in this limited excavation, and with such an important emphasis by me and others on the ritual use of rock-art in burials, there are so many outstanding questions that we need all the data we can get.

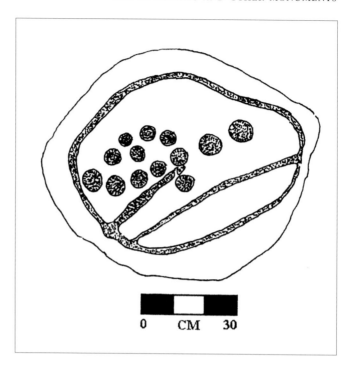

96 Fylingdales kerbstone.
Based on Paul Brown

0   CM   30

The press publicity that accompanied the revelation of the unique slab was different in tone from the more carefully considered results of excavation and comments of those who know about rock-art. One interesting aspect of this is that at a time when laser scanning is rightly being considered as an important, non-invasive means of recording rock-art, in this case Paul Brown's digital photographs were as good as anything produced by that method for publication purposes. Another very good result of this discovery was the sharing of information provided by those who have done extensive fieldwork with those whose jobs make them responsible for the excavation of sites and their preservation.

The fate of the decorated stones, of their being left in situ, is by no means shared by all, as it is thought that there is a threat from treasure-hunters. The alternative is to have a replica in situ and put the original in a museum where everyone can share it, because it is so important.

The other large kerbstone, originally reported by Barbara and Paul Brown and Graeme Chappell, had a roughly circular shape echoed by an inner groove that enclosed 13 cups and two linear grooves. There were five small stones with single cups, a larger one with a linear pattern and a polished stone with an oval depression in which were tiny pick-marks and a thin groove. The presence of smaller cup-marked stones in a mound is not unusual, as we have seen.

This concludes a look at cairn and barrow sites discovered over a hundred years ago and some of those excavated recently. The most important of the latter are in Scotland, Northumberland, County Durham and the North Yorkshire Moors. No doubt more will be excavated or re-excavated in order to seek further information (*colour plate 7*).

The rock-art at Allan Tofts, the nearest to Fylingdales, generally falls into the category of 'Art in the Landscape', or open-air. The site is on wide terraces on a hillside with extensive views, but there are stone and earth walls and about 120 small cairns, larger cairns and barrows (Brown and Chapell 2005). The presence of marked rocks among them, with their characteristic pattern of long parallel grooves, cup clusters and deep cups, linked cups and a grid pattern, could be linked closely with monuments. A similar scatter of marked rocks, usually earthfast boulders, is also found in Northumberland sites, especially at Chatton Sandyford, where some of the cairns have incorporated rock-art on small kerbstones.

There is another type of burial associated with carved stones: that in a pit with a small decorated stone over it. This type has been noted particularly in Northumberland, but only constitutes a small number.

STANDING STONES

Single or settings of standing stones are some of the most impressive monuments in Britain. As soon as a stone is 'planted' in its socket or wedged upright, it takes on an almost human life. Stonehenge, Avebury, Stenness, Brodgar and Swinside are some that spring to mind, shared by thousands of visitors. It is not unusual to find people with a rapt expression offering seeds, flowers or scattered earth to these stones. I remember one day finding a happy young Yorkshireman sitting on the grass with his back resting against one of the stones at Castlerigg playing a diggery-doo. He was touring as many stones as he could, enjoying his performance and getting a lot out of it.

Individual stones, too, are impressive, especially on the scale of the Devil's Arrows, close to the A1. People speculate on whether they have an astronomical significance, seeking alignments with other stones, prominent landscape features and the heavens. Here I am concerned with those that have motifs on them. We have seen how megaliths play a vital role in the architecture of passage-graves, where stones and symbols form an integral part in the way some are constructed. Now attention turns to stones that have cups, cups-and-rings, lines or spirals carved on their faces, marks which echo the whole idea of 'circularity' in the construction of monuments.

A good starting point is Long Meg and her Daughters (Beckensall 2002) for the impressive stone circle with its outlying pillar throws up a number of questions that dictate how we think about these circles in our attempts to understand what they were for and why that pattern was chosen (*colour plate 14*). Within the general area of Penrith, there is a concentration of henge monuments, some of the most impressive in Britain. Henges have received special attention in recent excavations. At Thornborough, Harding's excavations have produced more information about them, drawing on data from all over Britain in order to find out what place they had as the 'culmination of cultural achievement' during the Neolithic period (Harding 2003). Two surviving henges out of three near Penrith, at King Arthur's Round Table and the Mayburgh henge, are indicative of the importance of the circle in monuments, and of the importance of enclosing an area that must have been regarded as 'special'. At Long Meg we know of no henge, but we do know that the stone circle is part on a much more extensive complex of enclosed areas. One was a small stone circle reported by Stukeley in 1725, but now ploughed over. Aerial photography using infra-red film has captured two others, one a circle larger than the stone circle, abutting it to the north, with both circles flattened, and the other, a smaller one, to the east. There is another, south of Burstop Wood. It is important some day to discover the nature of these circular enclosures, as we know nothing more about them. From reports it is likely that the centre of Long Meg circle had barrows added, as at Temple Wood (K), but again this has to be verified.

Most drawings of Long Meg have been inadequate, and Simpson in the nineteenth century came closest to realising what was on that face. Since my own drawing the motifs have been laser-scanned. There are spirals, concentric arcs, lines, and a cup and concentric rings. It is likely that many of these motifs have been added at different times. Some are unfinished, as an arc of cups may have been intended to be joined together, for example, and others seem to jostle each other for position. I have described and illustrated this rock in detail elsewhere (Beckensall 2002) and have many digital images, prints and slides to back this up. The drawing may not be the last word, but it is considerably more detailed than anything offered before (Burl, 1999 pp.40-41). I still have not done the top metre. It will be of considerable interest if someone conducts a skilled excavation of the site to work out a sequence for all the features there.

We do have the outstanding fact that Long Meg is of a different material from the other stones, a red sandstone that probably came from a nearby cliff beside the River Eden. Whether it came before the circle, after, or was contemporary with it, we do not know. Were the motifs pecked on before it was raised into position? Were they already on when it was brought there? Were additions made, and if so over what period? Another recently discovered factor, made by Steven

Hood and Dave Hankin, observant non-professionals, is that one fallen standing stone on the flattened north part of the circle has a spiral and faint concentric arcs. Two other stones may have markings, but this is not definite. These are on volcanic rock, and would have been more difficult to peck than on sandstone. They reported these to me after catching the shadow at just the right time of day. Again, this emphasises the importance of visiting a site at different seasons and times of day, and reminds us that we may have missed other motifs. Other parts of the story, the legend of the witch and her daughters punished for dancing on the Sabbath, its announcement on the local signpost as a Druid's circle, and the story of men fleeing in terror when they were about to blow it up with gunpowder when a violent thunderstorm frightened the life out of them, are all indications of how people react to such an enigma. The site is a powerful and intriguing place, still largely unexplained, remaining still and large on its slight slope, with Long Meg herself at the highest part looking not only on the circle but at the whole landscape. Meanwhile, it is not enclosed with fences, but, as at Castlerigg, animals graze there, claiming the right to be there as much as we do.

At Temple Wood (K) the excavators were confronted by a similar problem, of sequencing not just one stone circle on the site, but two. Both are well displayed today, and the circle to the north proved to be earlier. This began life as a circle of wooden posts, later replaced by stones, although the building of this stone circle may have been abandoned. Attention moved to another circle built of 22 standing stones to the south-west. Both circles lie in an area of large burial cairns and standing stones within the Kilmartin valley. The second one was 'closed down' as a stone circle, side-slabs were placed between standing stones (one of them with two cup-marks), and the circle became a focus for Early Bronze Age cists and cairns. Thus the function of the stone circle changed to an area that enclosed burials. One of the standing stones has finely-made double spirals that are linked on two faces. Another has two concentric rings. What we do not know is at what moment they were put there, but their presence adds importance to the site (Scott 1989).

The Castlerigg stone circle (C) was examined in detail by Nick Best and Neil Stevenson who discovered markings on some of the stones, two of them lozenge-shapes, and one a spiral. I made rubbings of the spiral without actually being able to see it, and published a drawing which coincided with their photograph, but since then high-tech scanning has failed to locate it. Out of thousands of rocks that I have recorded in this way, this one has caused me worry! The lozenge-shapes and an arc and cup are visible (Beckensall 2002a). Others now claim to have found spiral grooves and have published images of it (e.g. 'Wolfy' on the Internet).

It does happen sometimes that rock-art is almost invisible; a good example is incorporated in the Glassonby circle (C), where the circle of stones, usually called a stone circle, is an oval kerb which encloses burials that may have covered different periods. Originally the kerb included two marked stones, one that has now disappeared since it was recorded in 1875, made of red sandstone that had 'a spiral or concentric circles'. The surviving stone, still in situ but hardly visible, was photographed at the time of discovery; it took a long time for me to record it, small though it is, as the markings are on a near-vertical face, but the pattern is very clear: faint linear marks, concentric rings, concentric semi-circles and three chevrons with the beginnings of a fourth near ground level.

There may have been cobbles covering cremations and a cist in the enclosed area, and there was an inverted urn outside the circle containing bones and charcoal, all pointing to a secondary use of the site in the Early Bronze Age (Beckensall 2002a).

As so many of the markings have been difficult to see, it is very important for all stones in monuments to be examined in different lights. Again, this makes a case for using laser technology which is not dependent on natural light.

In County Donegal there is a stone circle at Beltany, where five of the 65 standing stones have cup-marks, one heavily clustered, and one cup has a ring. Of five other decorated standing stones in the county, three are decorated on two faces. Cardonagh has four cups on the east face and 12 on the west. The Glebe Stone, with its rounded top, has 15 cups, two joined by a groove. Ardmoor is the

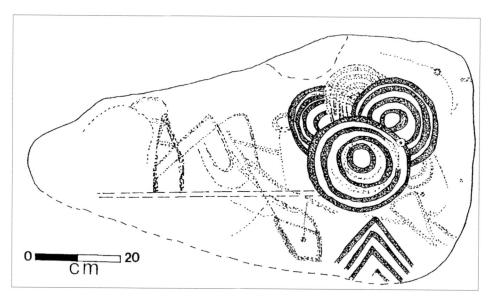

97 Glassonby kerbstone (C)

most elaborately decorated on its rectangular slab surface with cups and cups-and-rings. Barnes Lower South has on its west face three cups and on its east face a scatter of cups-and-rings, some joined by grooves. Barnes Lower North has east and west faces cup-marked, with a cross motif formed by linking two sets of cups on the west (van Hoek 1987, 1988).

Single and grouped standing stones with motifs are present in northern Britain. There is a particularly fine example at Balkemback Wood, near Tealing, Angus. Standing stones at this site are thought by some to be the remains of a 'four-poster', a setting common to Scotland with a burial at the centre, where if a decorated stone is included it is at the south-east. The choice of this particular stone in the group for motifs is interesting, since its most profusely decorated face is the most difficult to cope with, having so many irregularities. Other surfaces are smooth (red sandstone conglomerate); this choice of the east face is determined by what we find so often in British rock-art: the design was already suggested by the shape of the stone and its irregular surface features. Usually rock-art takes advantage of what is already there, so cracks, undulations, slope and other natural features direct the design. This one was already pitted with natural cups and other indentations, and its outline appears to us to be closest to a human shape (although they may not have seen it that way).

Two other surfaces of the same rock have been marked; the east with cups and connected cups, and the north with possible cup-marks.

A key element in the design on the east face is the long groove on the south edge that begins with a natural crack at the top and continues parallel to the edge all the way down. Seven grooves run into this, roughly parallel to one another, from the north, some from cups and cups-and-rings all on the same plane.

The vertical groove has a deep and two shallower parallel grooves on the north side. This forms a rectangle that frames most of motifs on the rock. Another major groove, beginning at the same top (S) corner runs obliquely across the rectangle, but when it reaches a natural fault in the surface, it changes direction, curving towards the south. The large cup at the top north of the rectangle has another groove running away to the north edge. The enclosed motifs are six cups-and-rings, two touching, and two linked by a groove through the central cups. It is highly unlikely that the stone was decorated when it was standing; it would have been decorated when it lay flat.

This smoother west face has 27 cups, mostly quite large, with some connected by grooves. Five cups are interconnected at the south-west corner. There are four cups arranged in an arc below one another, with two beside them connected by a groove. Two other cups are linked by a groove, and three have a faint groove connecting them in an arc downwards. One cup at the bottom has a groove.

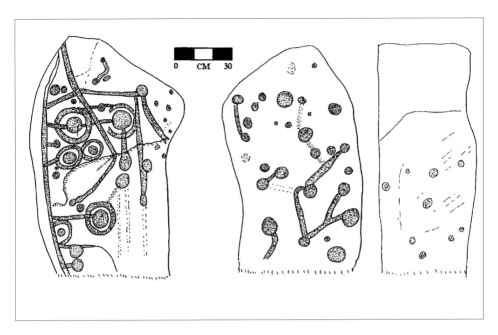

98 Balkemback (Angus) stone decorated on three faces

99 Balkemback, Angus

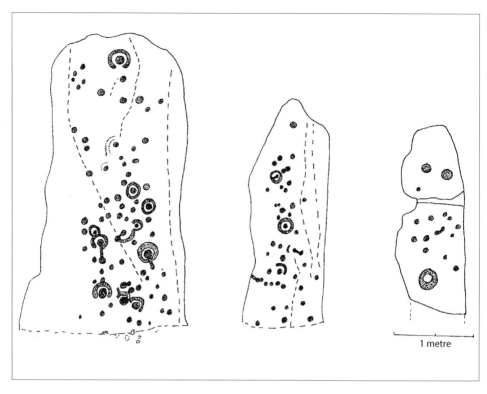

100 Ballymeanoch (K); three of seven standing stones are decorated

The north face is difficult to assess, as there are apparently cup-marks, but it is hard to say which are natural. How the site would have appeared originally is not easy to visualise. The colour of grass and the surface suggest that there may have been sockets for other standing stones, and the whole site needs a geophysical assessment to establish this. It appears to be at the end of a slightly raised track into the settings, but again this is speculative. It is important to pursue this further in order to establish the full significance of prehistoric rock-art on standing stones, as indeed it is in the whole of Britain. It may not be a four-poster.

Sometimes standing stones are isolated, and often become the subject of folklore or associated with events that they considerable pre-dated. Northumberland has a few: at Matfen, Swinburne, and The Warrior Stone at Ighoe and a small, beautifully positioned small stone circle, one of which has cup-marks, at Duddo (Beckensall 2001).

The best group of marked standing stones is in the Kilmartin Glen (Beckensall 2005). The Ballymeanoch Standing stones share an area containing other prehistoric monuments including a henge, burials of different periods and decorated outcrop, on a terrace (Beckensall 2005).

They are very impressive and create a special atmosphere with their stillness, arrangement, size and setting. Of particular interest are three with motifs. Originally seven in number in settings of two parallel lines of four and two, there are six standing; one fell down over 100 years ago, the stump was excavated and its remains were dumped close to a kerbed cairn (*colour plate 17*).

The line of four stones has the tallest to the north. The next south is extensively decorated on its flat, rectangular east face. The motifs seem to follow the line of an oblique crack. They are mostly well-finished cups; some have partial rings or arcs and three have ducts running from the ringed cups into a single cup. Some of the cups are known to lie below the present field level. The next stone south is also decorated, this time on the west face, with mostly cups, some linked by a groove. At the pointed top of the stone is a cup with a faint ring. There is a prominent cup at the centre of an ungapped ring in the middle of the stone, and two touching cups at the centre of a ring between the two.

Many of the cups cluster together, and are linked to one another. The third standing stone with markings, now lying half buried by the kerbed cairn, stood 18m west-north-west of the more northerly of the pair of stones that lie roughly parallel to the four. It is curiously decorated, the most prominent feature being an hourglass perforation that runs right through the stone face. Below that are small cups, two joined by a groove, but the top part has two large cups that look like eyes. No doubt this is how they would have appeared to people visiting the site in the past. But what of the hole? Did people have to look through it? At what? The stone stood in a pit that had three small patches of cremated bone in it. Was this some sort of foundation deposit? Was it human bone? These seven stones make up part of a large complex of standing stones in Kilmartin Glen. What was the significance of their alignments? Had it anything to do with astronomy? Were they used in some dance-like ceremony? Were they pointing people in the direction of something important or away from something to be avoided? We will never know, but can speculate endlessly. Why not? They make good stories, and the stones and theories belong to all of us.

Crossing Kilmartin Glen north-westwards one is confronted by a similar group of standing stones, the Nether Largie Standing Stones, one of which is similarly cup-and-ring marked.

The stones are aligned north-east and south-west, with two paired stones at each end of the alignment. In between are settings of four and five stones. There is another one 100m (an 'outlier') from the north end of the alignment. The stump of another was excavated in 1973, 300m west of the south end (another outlier), but was covered over again. The decorated stone dominates a setting of five stones, centred on two pairs of flankers, of which only three are in position.

101 Nether Largie (K): an elaborate setting of standing stones, some decorated

The stone is 2.8m high, roughly rectangular in shape with an oblique piece broken off the top. Two cracks run down from top to bottom and join near the base. To the right are 12 cups spread out from top to bottom. Four cups are hammered into the left crack; between the two cracks are cups, some with ducts, and a cup-and-ring. In the left part are two cups with a duct each at the centre of penannulars, one penannular ending in a cup. Seventeen cups, two with ducts, make up the rest, including four at the base. The decorated stone adds importance in its setting, not only for its size and relationship to the rest of the standing stones, but the fact that it has this decoration to distinguish it. To the north-east of the setting is a pair of standing stones. Close by, to the north-west, is a setting of four followed by paired stones 24m away. It is like a long rectangle with two stones at each end and two sets of diamond-shaped settings between them.

Again, the stones are not in isolation, but part of a 'ritual' landscape that includes a Clyde cairn, round cairns, cists with axe motifs and two stone circles at Temple Wood (Beckensall 2005). This is one of the most important valleys for prehistoric remains in Britain, and rock-art takes its place there.

This section concludes with the results of two important series of excavations that examine monuments which combine both stone circles and burials.

There are in North-East Scotland two types of distinctive monument known as Clava Cairns and Recumbent Stone Circles. Some cairns at Clava have been excavated by Richard Bradley, and recently three recumbent stone circles have been excavated in a project headed by him, with much expertise involved, all published to the highest standards (Bradley 2005). This contrasts with years of neglect of many of the Scottish sites deplored by Alexander Keiller, who told the British Association in 1934:

> I feel an unhappy duty must devolve upon me as representing, in some sort, on this occasion, local archaeology, and that is to apologise, in all sincerity and bitterness of heart, for the condition in which those who have travelled to Aberdeen will find our ancient monuments. (1934, p.22)

People spoke and wrote of the appalling appearance of so many monuments, using words like 'squalid, unkempt, dirty, disgusting'.

This pushed many monuments into guardianship, since when there has been a considerable improvement, and the excavation of Tomnaverie, Cothiemuir Wood and Aikey Brae has not only revealed, as part of a series of investigations since Keiller's words, more about these monuments, but allowed one of them to be reinstated for public access. Two of them have cup-marks incorporated.

Recumbent stone circles are so-called because a major focus in their design is a large horizontally-placed stone slab between two large upright monoliths as part of a circle. The excavation of Tomnaverie has established that the first structure on the site was a ring-cairn – a circle of stones, or rather a polygon – and that this became part of a planned sequence that was based on a constructed flat platform, leading to the realignment of its kerb to include the recumbent stone and its flankers, with monoliths arranged in a ring concentric to it, also on the platform. The section that included the recumbent and flankers was a long, straight section. The use of different coloured stones in the various stages of construction is important, notably the whitish stone of the recumbent, emphasising that this was the focus. The cup-marks, the most basic in rock-art, are significantly pecked on the recumbent and on three kerbstones. Within the landscape on the 170m OD hill are four cup-marked outcrops and three boulders, with many other marked rocks, especially to the north on lower ground, although the report does not illustrate them.

The Loanhead of Daviot has a cupped stone east of the flanker, and the Sunhoney circle has a large cluster of cups on the top surface of the recumbent. Such recumbent stone blocks exist in Ireland as part of passage-graves, but not elsewhere.

The second circle excavated as part of the project was Cotheimuir Wood, where the cup-marks on the recumbent stone are on its outer face, clustered around

102 Tomnaverie recumbent standing stone circle in 1993, since excavated and reinstated

veins of quartzite in the stone. The monument had the same kind of structure as Tomnaverie, a kerb with stones packed into it enclosing a central space, this time with a slab in the middle covering some sort of pit, and the erection of possibly 12 monoliths around the kerb, including the recumbent and its flankers. All had been built on top of a flat hill with wide views. Again the choice of material and its colour are important to the construction: kerbstones alternate between red and grey slabs, and so do the monoliths. The flankers are pink, the recumbent grey to white, with its inclusion of quartz. One flanker is pointed, the other flat-topped.

Richard Bradley also conducted meticulous excavations on Clava Cairns, and again I concentrate on those in his report which have cups and cup-and-ring markings incorporated in their structures.

The Balnuaran of Clava is a linear cemetery built on a gravel terrace flanking the River Nairn which contains passage-graves surrounded by standing stones, a ring-cairn and a kerb-cairn. They had been thought to belong to different periods, and the passage-grave was thought to be derived from those in Ireland, at roughly the same date. The results of excavation have turned these suppositions on their heads, as all the monuments have proved to be of the same period, the

Early Bronze Age, which is considerably later than those in Ireland. The rock-art incorporated in the monuments is of the cup-and-ring type, with nothing of the exotic curvilinear designs that we see in the Irish passage-graves. Some cup-marks and rings had already been recorded before the excavators discovered more, some of them hidden at the time of construction. All the monuments share a special use of different coloured stone, ranging from red to white, and most of them include cup-marks as part of their construction.

The two passage-graves, already well-restored and visited, are very much alike. Both have a roughly circular inner chamber defined by blocks of stone that support horizontal dry-stone walling leading to corbelling for a small roof, with a passage leading out to the platform on which a kerbed-cairn of boulders and cobbles has been constructed to include all these features. Circling the passage-grave is a ring of spaced standing stones. A notable feature of both passage-graves is that the height of the stones is graded, with a focal point of the smallest at the back of the chamber.

Four cairns are on display to the public, although the cemetery extends further. From west to east, in order, there is the south-west passage-grave, a small kerbed-cairn, a central ring-cairn and the north-east passage-grave. Excavations were precise and limited to answer questions about structure and particularly about chronology, supported by field-walking and by intensive documentary research. It was a typical example of its kind.

I shall summarise the different features, concentrating on where rock-art fits in. The central ring-cairn has a wall of cobbles held in by an outer and inner kerb, around what looks today to be a central empty space. With the smallest at the north-east, the stones are graded in size. There is a low platform outside the outer kerb and a ring of standing stones outside it, originally 11, but now nine. Three of them are joined to the outer kerb by rubble banks, referred to as 'rays'; where one of these rays meets the outer kerb, two of these kerbs are cup-marked. One standing stone of banded gneiss has a cup on its outer face, and a possible faint one on its opposite. There is another on one of the tallest stones of the inner kerb.

A kerb that had fallen inwards was exposed by excavation, at the junction of the ray, with well-made cups covering its surface, down to its base and underside. The south-west passage-grave has cup and cup-and-ring-marked stones, some of which were discovered during this new investigation. Red sandstone is a particularly important choice for them and in the structure generally. One flat-topped monolith in front of the cairn has three cups on its inner face. Towards the back of the monument is a cupped sandstone slab that continues below the surface of the platform.

The excavation revealed that when the chamber floor was uncovered, cup-marks were found buried. Of great interest is the discovery of cups on stones that

Above: 103 Balnuaran of Clava: passage-grave

Opposite: 104 Clava cairns: the ring-cairn

had been laid horizontally on the orthostats at the back of the chamber, three built like a dry-stone wall with one, two and seven cup-marks. Another rests on top of the orthostat.

The north-east passage-grave is similar in structure to the south-west, with two slabs on the north side of the central passage, one of which has rings too. Only one cup was recorded in the corbelling, which again is a horizontally-built dry-stone wall.

The most highly-decorated stone on the whole site is a kerb at the back, with well-defined pecked cups enclosed by grooves arranged to zone the slab, including a cup-and-ring. It is unlikely that the stone was ever exposed for long, and must have been protected by cairn material.

The conclusion was that 'there is little evidence that carvings of rings and cup-and-rings are associated with the primary phases of this monument', but there was little time lapse between one phase and another.

The kerb-cairn, the smallest monument, badly damaged, has its stones arranged in size and by colour, with a block of red sandstone forming a 'threshold', covered with cups. The whole of these structures is now thought to have been conceived as a set of monuments from the beginning.

The site bore some signs of having been used as a settlement before the monuments were built, as cereals such as barley were grown there; it could be that the cemetery was built close to a settlement and that some of the building material could have been reused, some possibly coming from clearance of boulders and cobbles when the ground was prepared for cultivation and pasture. The cupped stones could have already been there, but as building of all the structures took place at the same time, generally, they could be more or less

contemporary. The general sequence for monument building was *c.*1950-1870 BC, the Early Bronze Age, usually associated with Food Vessels, Beakers and distinctive artefacts although field-walking found a wider range. There appear to be very few burials; there is a contrast between the number of people buried there and the number of people required for the building! It has been estimated that a passage-grave here needed *c.*3000 worker-hours to build.

When all the Clava cairns are examined in their settings, they extend from 70km east–west to 50km north–south, with a concentration to the south and east of Inverness along the Nairn and Spey valleys. They are generally in low-lying areas near rivers, mostly on valley floors. The areas are inconspicuous and could have been used for settlement.

Perhaps the most astonishing fact of the excavations was that of the 33 dates, not one was Neolithic. They are therefore in a different tradition from the passage-graves of Ireland, later, regional, and are not built up over a long period of time. Other Scottish passage-graves do not have cup-marks (yet!), and they are confined to the open-air and to standing stones so it looks as though there is a link in time. In the recumbent stone circles, as we have seen, they are thought to be associated with the phases of the moon.

A comparable area where markings are made is in the Kilmartin Glen, where the large round cairns are not Neolithic, though it is always possible that they lie on more ancient sites. Another comparison is that both linear cemeteries are on routes through great glens of considerable importance. Clava is at a pivotal point.

7

Portable art

'Portable' rock-art means that the rock has been removed from its original position. I have recorded marked stones built into kitchen walls, rockeries, field walls, stone heaps, and even three embedded in concrete foundations supporting an eighteenth-century bridge at Wallington Hall (N) and another in the foundations of the hall of Prudhoe Castle (N).

It is obvious that there are some outcrop quarries from which slabs have been removed, leaving motifs that have been sheared through. Some quarries have prehistoric rock-art still there, but this may also be alongside picked-out outlines of millstones, spaces where they have been removed, and some still in situ awaiting the final severance. By 'portable' we mean that the stone can be carried. In a sense a marked stone removed from one monument to another is portable.

In Northumberland alone there are many of these, and all over Britain they have been discovered, especially recently now that people know where to look. The exercise of examining a field wall near to cairns or the sites of cairns, in favourable light, has led to the discovery of many pieces of rock-art.

Other discoveries may be in more obvious places, such as a large flat-topped decorated boulder that sits on top of a Roman wall at Coria (N), with an enclosure of many cups.

Another smaller cup-and-ring-marked stone is embedded in a cobbled pavement outside the Bay Horse Hotel at Ravensworth (D). Museums hold many, some of them unprovenanced and neglected. Many are in store where they can only be seen by researchers, such as those in the Museum of Antiquities, Newcastle, although there are plans for these to be displayed adequately when the new Great North Museum is built. Even some of those on show elsewhere are squeezed in and not well displayed. The display of rock-art has not been considered a priority or even an essential component of the archaeological record until now. These portables are too numerous to list here, but each major rock-art area has some.

105 Portable stone in a wall at Ravenhall (NYM). *Paul Brown*

In Angus and Dundee there are some portables located in souterrains, perhaps 1500 years earlier than the structures themselves, which are banana-shaped underground cold storehouses of the Iron Age. One can imagine people looking around for building material, seeing these decorated stones, and using them in their building, but their placement appears more than casual. At Tealing, the 'earth house' has a design of pleasant complexity on a boulder that was used as a foundation of the souterrain inner wall. Another decorated rock on the same site is embedded in grass (part of the reconstructed top), covered with cups.

Other souterrains with rock-art in Angus and Dundee are: Airlie, with a serpentine decoration; Pitcur, with a ring; Carlungie, with cup-and-ring; and Ardestie, with cup-and-ring.

In some instances marked rock appears in enclosures built later than the Bronze Age. For example, the Hugill Iron Age settlement in Cumbria (Beckensall 2002a) has a wall enclosing hut circles and smaller walled-off areas. Some of the rock was quarried nearby to make the enclosures, and it is possible that the quarry surface included cup-marks, for some of these have found their way into the walls. The placement is not random, as two of the largest cup-marked stones were placed on the inner face of the enclosing wall facing each other at opposite points across the enclosure.

106 Tealing souterrain (Angus) has two reused decorated stones

Above: 107 Ruckcroft (C) portable

Right: 108 Deershed (N) portable

109 Penrith Museum: two decorated cobbles and the Stag Stone Farm slab

In the same county there are some other interesting portables, distinguished by the quality of the decoration. One found at Ruckcroft, Armathwaite is a flattish, triangular local sandstone cobble with its decoration centred on a cup, nicely symmetrical and partly smoothed, with a duct running from the apex of the triangle, with two concentric penannulars added (Beckensall 2002 pp.127-9). It is very much like one from Deershed Plantation, Northumberland. Both stones must have been displaced.

Another, from Stag Stone Farm (C), is a slab with pristine markings, found at the base of a drystone wall during gas pipe excavations (ibid. 125).

A cobble in Penrith Museum has cups an two sides, and a similar one was found recently at Crosby Ravensworth (C) by John and Nicola Bisset with both stones illustrated here.

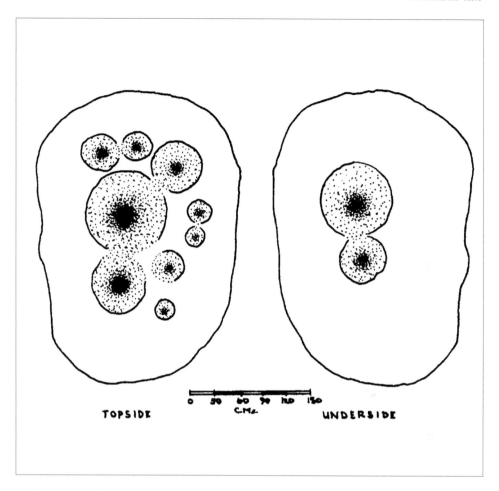

110 Decorated cobble from Crosby Ravensworth (C). *Drawing: J. Bisset*

Another particularly well-executed design comes from Dean Church (C) (ibid.). In contrast to these is a much larger block covered with complex art from Honey Pots Farm, now in Tullie House Museum, Carlisle, taken by lorry there from where it lay above the banks of the River Eamont (Beckensall 2002a pp.131-3).

It is not possible to say how the stones end up where they do, although some are so attractive that they make good museum exhibits. One gratifying aspect of all this is that more people are beginning to look for them and record them, and ensure that they are safely housed. Brown and Chappell (2005), for example, have discovered many on the North York Moors. Although it is generally good procedure to leave things where they are found, the result of leaving portables is that they can be used to repair walls or roads or be taken off to display in someone's garden. If there is any danger of this happening, they should be moved to a place of safety.

A sign of the times is that in a recent article by Darvill and Wainwright (PPS 69, 2003, pp.253-64) the article begins with the report of a discovery of a humble cup-marked stone on the verge of an unclassified road in Wales. Given the name Dan-Y-Garn stone, it was measured, laser-scanned and described in detail with a whole page for the scan. It is the start of an article that lists all Welsh rock-art and relates it to the rest of Britain. This is thorough and encouraging, although the laser scanning of one small stone may seem to some a sledge hammer to crack a nut. It seems that the less there is of anything in the archaeological record, the more is said about it (especially when we see pages of drawings of rather undistinguished flints). However, the recording of marked cobbles is particularly important, as examples in situ are closely related to round barrow and cairn construction.

About terminology: I prefer to call these stones 'portable' as they were carried there by people. 'Mobiliary' rather amusingly suggests that they move under their own steam; the stuff of legend, no doubt like standing stones going to drink at the river. (Is this a phenomenon or is it phenomenological?)

An intriguing discovery in the grounds of Ashford Primary School, Derbyshire, was of two large, flat Millstone Grit boulders with elaborate decoration (Barnatt and Robson 2003) which were found when heavy machines moved many large boulders from the eastern end of a football pitch. The stones lay in a corner of the field until they were needed for the development of an 'environmental garden' and pond, when the markings were first noticed. The interest generated among adults and children was enormous. At a later stage a third faintly-decorated boulder, already near the gate to the school car park, was also saved. These were among 35-40 boulders moved during landscaping; two which are so large that they could not have been moved easily are decorated only on one face and have plough scratch marks on the same face, as well as other damage. They may have become 'portable' in a sense, but are likely to have been earthfast when they were decorated and, from the freshness of the picking, have been covered over by this soil soon after the motifs were added.

The motifs on the two larger stones are unusual; the first rock has angular rings centred on cups, but the penannulars flanking the groove running from the central cup curl into a simple spiral, echoed by another spiral outside the rings. There is interconnection of motifs by linear grooves. The second rock is very unusual: again, spirals end an encircling groove around a serpentine, coiled pattern. Other apparently tentative figures are curved grooves, with a large cup and penannular. The third, badly damaged, has two cups enclosed by penannulars.

The site, on a gently-sloping valley shelf above the River Amber, may have been on a route for animals moving to and from pastures, but not much is known

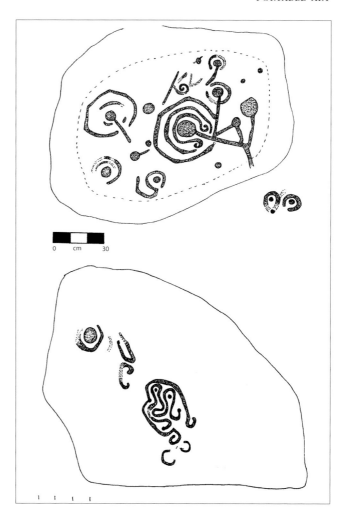

0 cm 30

111 Ashford Primary School stones (P)

about the area in prehistoric times. Although I have included the site in the 'portable' section, it is likely that these boulders were moved only recently, and originally were earthfasts.

One other portable is an almost purely Scottish phenomenon: the decorated stone ball. Almost 400 have been found between the Moray Firth and the River Tay. There is an overspill, as two have now been found in Northumberland, one on a Neolithic settlement site in 2005 on the Milfield plain (Waddington, forthcoming). Some of the balls are plain, and some have incredibly skilful decoration, like those found at Skara Brae in the Neolithic domestic site. These would appear to be of that date, but some analysts think that although most could have been made with a stone tool, others required metal ones. Their purpose in unclear, but considering the amount of time that was put into their

112 Carved ball, *c.* 8cm diameter from Monzie, Aberdeenshire. *Royal Museums of Scotland, with permission of the Trustees*

manufacture they must have been something worth having. Some of the most intricate have spiral patterns carved on them but, as we know, spirals are not confined to an early prehistoric period. Their use must for the moment remain a mystery, but they could have been a must-have accessory rather like a polished axe from Langdale.

8

Layers of meaning

In trying to understand what rock-art means, we must not only acquire as much data as possible, but also we must always keep a sense of proportion; as with so much in the past, we have probably lost a great amount, and tend to make generalisations from what is left. If rock-art is used over at least a thousand years, we have indeed a tiny representation to scatter over that period, like a little sand on a field. The sum total of what we know best has to be examined carefully and added to our knowledge of rock-art in the rest of Britain and indeed in the rest of the world.

Although we know that many questions that we raise cannot be answered, this must not make us forget that we do know a considerable amount about it, enabling us to draw some conclusions. This chapter draws together facts and interpretations from the rest of the book to show the reader what stage we have reached in our thinking. I use the pronoun 'we' to include many I know who are involved in the research and share at least some of my conclusions.

In attempting some sort of synthesis, I have to begin by asking myself many questions. Will the collection of more data enable archaeologists to draw conclusions about what the motifs mean, or do we already have sufficient information to make a judgement? Are we any further along the road to understanding than the antiquarians of the nineteenth century who became fascinated by the phenomenon? Does my knowledge of so many areas and detailed familiarity with the panels and single marked stones put me in a better position than anyone else to offer a hypothesis? Am I aware of the significance of what I already know? Do the insights that I have gained from a variety of sources allow me to deal with the relationships between the types of motifs made, the landscapes where they occur and the contexts of burials and monuments where some of them are found? How much of my cultural background will help or get in the way of understanding something of the minds of people who lived over 4000 years ago?

Is there a danger of transferring knowledge of other cultures that used symbols as paintings, etchings and pecked-out designs on rock surfaces to those of Britain? How far is analogy useful and how far misleading? How far can developments in disciplines related to archaeology such as science, aesthetics, psychology and philosophy help us to understand rock-art? Changes in emphasis in all these disciplines, refutation of one idea and substitution by another should warn us that our own conclusions will certainly be questioned, and that we must make the effort to hypothesise and open ourselves up to challenges now or in the future.

In studying rock-art we are drawn deeply into motives for human behaviour thousands of years ago. The spread, context and frequency of motifs alert us to their importance in the prehistoric world. The fact that 'geometric' shapes rather than pictures of people and animals are exclusive subjects tells us that something is being taken out of the 'natural' world and represented in a powerful kind of shorthand. The process of abstracting such important symbols comes from the mind, either through observation of something in nature or from some deeply-rooted built-in imagery. Consciousness or awareness of the world does not come merely by observing it and living in it or by using intelligence to solve problems. Strong feelings play an important part in the way we think and how we perceive the world. The mind can be heightened by excitement, and we learn and create not just in a state of cold reason but by being excited. In our dreams a world partly 'real' and a world created and imaginary comes to the surface; their revelations can be very disturbing and bring up many of our anxieties. The apparently simplest of human emotions are the most difficult to articulate, and poets may choose analogy to create 'layers of meaning'. Words themselves arranged in a pattern produce sounds that not only convey meaning but also some of the sensation that gives rise to that feeling – so that it can be strongly expressed. It is possible to understand a poem without knowing exactly what it means. Perhaps the poet doesn't know either, otherwise it might have been written in another way, such as prose. The writer may not be fully conscious of the implications of everything that has been written, and the reader or listener may get something from it that is unique to him or her.

In prehistoric art, 'pictures' of animals, places and human activities may carry far more meaning to the people who made them and to those who saw them than to us. When cave paintings were first discovered in Europe they were so vivid that people at first refused to believe that they could possibly be so old; they had preconceived ideas that 'savages' were incapable of such art. This idea has changed; those who painted such images in caves are now thought by some to have done so when they had visions through which they acquired the images that they depicted, so that animals took on a much greater significance than something to be hunted and eaten. The idea of people painting such images because they had plenty of time to do so was also rejected along with the concept of 'art for art's sake'. This type of art was fundamental to a whole view of life that was so important that it was expressed in dangerous, narrow and confined spaces underground where perhaps only a few people would ever see it, and only with the help of lights carried down there. A question that arises is: why are some animals well-represented, and not others?

The 'meaning' of such images continues to be explored with questions such as: why are there so many dots? What characteristics of the animals are singled out specially, and why? Were they made by people with special powers and perceptions? Were such perceptions rooted firmly in human brains since *Homo sapiens* emerged? How were such perceptions brought from the depths to the surface of human minds? What did it all mean?

Having established that people who lived thousands of years ago were capable of expressing their perceptions of the real and spirit world so vividly in their art, this capability is certainly possible amongst any group of humans in the world, and certainly in Neolithic Britain.

If we view cup-and-ring art with this in mind, and give prehistoric people credit for coming to terms not only with survival in a hunting and farming world, they are also to be credited with being 'spiritual' beings.

FACING THE WORLD AND OUR OWN MINDS

Some people enjoy going into caves and will even crawl through narrow tunnels to explore underground; a place that is a source of mystery and appeals to their sense of adventure. Others find this claustrophobic, a threat, something that can induce panic with the idea of being shut in. Even Thor Heyerdahl found his courage leave him as he crawled after island guides in an underground tunnel on Easter Island; there seemed to be no going back or forward at one point. I remember in Malta following one of my teenage students as he swam through an underground tunnel. I did this without thinking, without using my imagination, but as the end seemed never to be coming I felt panic; there was enormous relief as we surfaced in a small cavern where there was air and light. Going back along the same route was no problem as I knew what to expect.

The effect of experiencing 'art' in caves or in man-made caves is quite different from looking at it in the open. The body is restricted, and so is the mind, when the space is a small one, for the senses may have to face real fears, to contemplate something awesome and unknown in both place and mind. Perhaps this is why such places were chosen for art: to contemplate the mystery, to face fear, to be initiated into dealing with our deep natures. The place is vital. The addition of images within the place directs attention to the things that other people want us to observe, to share the vision of, or in, a subterranean world.

Many mystics may not have chosen caves for their meditation, but the choice of desert place, of isolation and hardship, is common. The Gospels record how Jesus went into the wilderness to free himself, to be tempted. The lack of creature comforts for a long time would have made his mind receptive to what lay beneath the surface, to find out truly who he was. John the Baptist took a similar path before him, ate locusts and honey, dressed himself in animal skins, and came out with a missionary vision to warn the 'whited sepulchres' to repent before it was too late. When he baptised Jesus, despite his protests that he was unworthy, the Christian Church accepted a potent symbol of the dove, the Holy Spirit, descending on Jesus' head, present today on hundreds of stained-glass windows, and linking with the pre-Christian dove from Noah's ark which brought signs of life and the assurance that the flood was truly over. On many greetings cards it is accompanied by the word 'Peace'. Jesus had resisted the temptations to worldly power, to use it as a kind of magic trick, for his exercise of power was to be humble, self-effacing, a complete surrender to a higher will.

Many paintings show us mystics contemplating a skull, for what greater mystery is there than what happens after death? Loneliness and deprivation are key elements in contemplation; initiates into mysteries may have to tread that path if they are to go beyond the ordinary.

Coming to terms with the 'laws' of nature is a difficult process. If we consider the fact that all existence for the animal and insect world is based upon being part of a food chain, and that many 'nature' programmes seem to take great delight in showing us how cleverly creatures have adapted to attract and catch their prey, we realise that they have no choice in the matter. We humans do, to some extent, understand these laws and the complexities inherent in food chains although modern people can hardly form the same relationship with a tin of corned beef, a string of sausages or other form of food that does its best to hide from us what these things really are. For the primitive hunter there may have been no conflict, no choice, but their relationship was something to do with a warm, breathing creature which they may have admired for its grace, strength and beauty, yet were forced to hunt and use for food and clothing.

THE SHAPE OF THE WORLD AND OUR SENSE OF PLACE

This book is entitled 'Circles in Stone', which includes more than cups-and-rings hammered into stone. The whole created universe of the Neolithic/Early

113 Castlelerigg stone circle (C)

Bronze Age appears to be circular when it comes to what mattered most to them. Their early houses were rectangular, but before that a Mesolithic house on the North-East coast, in use for about 200 years, was round. Later Neolithic houses were circular in plan, and this remained the norm until the Roman occupation, when they stamped their own geometry into the landscape. Just think of all the monuments so often visited today: Stonehenge, Avebury, Silbury Hill, Maes Howe, the stone circles of Cumbria, recumbent stone circles in northern Scotland, the line of henges at Thornborough and smaller ones buried under the Milfield Plain. They are a fraction of circles built out of earth, stone and timber. Thousands of trees were felled, thousands of man-hours used to select materials and to construct these monuments, with the simplest of non-metal tools. Special offerings were made, such as Grooved Ware pottery, weapons, peoples' and animals' bones and ashes. Hundreds of long mounds, megalithic chambered tombs, cairns of stone and earth that housed the dead lie within this landscape.

Stand inside a circular open-air monument and you may feel partially enclosed, perhaps privileged to be 'on the inside'. Stand outside, and you may feel excluded or allowed to watch activities inside from a distance. Look carefully at the position of these rings of stone and you become aware that they may have been focal points for scattered communities as a meeting place, for they needed a shared identity, a common ancestry, a place to trade, a place to celebrate common beliefs and practices. More so than the circles of wood and stone, the burial mounds contained the dead, with fragments of their lives in the form of tools, weapons, ornaments, pottery and perhaps clothing. We still need places where the ancestors are, thus the visits to cemeteries to leave flowers or the burial of cremated bodies near homes or places special to the living and dead. Despite the modern insistence on our equality in the face of death, the monuments in graveyards belie this, for many give the impression that wealth and status will follow them into death.

It has been demonstrated that many stone and wood circles and henges are aligned to events such as the midsummer or midwinter solstice, some even believing that Stonehenge was a giant calendar. I do not for a moment think that prehistoric farmers needed stone alignments to tell them when to plant or harvest their crops; they lived so close to the land that experience and common sense told them how to manage it. But, just as today people have harvest festivals, there is a need to express gratitude to something or someone on whom farmers depend, for deliverance from things which they cannot control, such as drought, floods, sickness and other natural catastrophes.

If we live in a world where our ancestors have a real spiritual and even physical presence, where we may bury them under the floors of our houses, and where we build non-utilitarian structures involving us and our followers in a great deal of time and energy, we are acknowledging that we have to make efforts to get the gods and other manifestations of extra-terrestrial power on our side. The importance of such houses of the dead is that they may outnumber what remains of substantial domestic housing. In one sense they were useless; in another they were essential.

A sense of place and the power of places was strong in prehistoric communities. Today we mostly buy our food ready-packed. Farmers drive tractors to plough, harrow, sow, fertilise and harvest the land without the need to come into direct contact with the soil, and may live in another world brought through the music they listen to on their headphones as they do so. It's different for hill-farmers. Intimate first-hand knowledge of the land was crucial to survival and to the production of a surplus. If we are right about the period in which rock-art was made and used, it was at a time when agriculture was well established, but with a strong dependency still on hunting, pasturing animals and collecting food in the wild. Farming made people more settled in one place, involving clearance, fencing, building houses. Boundaries became more rigid. Pastoralism and hunting demanded more mobility, as they continued to do so for centuries afterwards, indeed in Britain the Shielings still remain as part of this seasonal life, when herdsmen went with their animals into the marginal lands where there was grazing and water. They may have followed well-tested routes and had marked territorial areas to avoid clashes with neighbours over grazing. Many of these grazing areas were also used for the burial of the dead, and it is possible that there was no distinction between the 'ritual' landscape of their stone circles and the sacred nature of the whole landscape, for what gives life and sustains it is sacred.

In more recent times, as I have discovered from my intensive study of Northumberland Field-Names (Beckensall 2006), another sign of the strong relationship between local communities and their land was expressed in the way in which they named their fields individually, socialising them, often incorporating a sense of humour, drawing attention to the land's fertility, or lack of it, to birds, beasts flowers and crops. We are losing this intimate relationship with our fields, and names such as these may disappear unless we record them: Boggle Hole, Labour in Vain, Standing Stone Close, High Seas, Corney Horners, Fislebee Pasture, Great and Little Sloshes, Featherblow.

Art in the landscape does not, however, give us a chronology. This has to come from its firm association with datable finds, in the same context either through scientific means or through pottery and artefact typologies.

Some stone circles incorporate rock-art, but in such a small minority of sites that one must be careful not to generalise. Although Long Meg (C) is covered with motifs on one face, the site is so complex and unexcavated that it is difficult or impossible to decide a definite sequence there. There are isolated standing stones, like those at Kilmartin, in alignments, but again it is not possible to date the rock-art precisely.

In burial mounds and in passage-graves we are, so to speak, on safer ground provided they have been thoroughly excavated using modern methods. The difference in the use of rock-art in the open-air from that in burials is significant, for in the latter not all of it is meant to be seen, and in passage-graves some of it perhaps seen only by a limited number of people, whereas the cairns seem to be finally closed as soon as the burial has been made. Some passage-graves show signs of having been re-opened periodically and reused. Another consideration for dating is that a piece of decorated rock can be transferred from one monument to another, but this dates the last use of that piece of decorated rock, not the grave itself. Even so, its use shows that the particular symbols on it are revered by those who have made the deliberate transfer. When a piece of rock is made specifically for the burial, either in the cist or in the material of the cairn itself we can definitely relate the date of that carving to the date of the burial through artefacts or radiocarbon dating.

Some sites combine stone circles and burials. With the recent excavation of the Clava Cairns we have learnt more about the position of rock-art in burials and monuments. These 'cairns' take the form of passage-graves, but occupy the same site as a kerbed-cairn and a ring-cairn. All these monuments are proved

114 Temple Wood stone circle, Kilmartin

from radiocarbon dating to be of the same age, and are hundreds of years later than the Irish passage-graves which they were once thought to echo. Not only is simple rock-art incorporated, some of it not meant to be seen, but also there is a deliberate grading of stone sizes and the use of colour. Similarly, the decoration of some standing stones throughout Britain may well belong to a period later than the Neolithic.

HOW AND WHY?

The big question remains of *why* rock was used in the places where we find it, whether landscape or in monuments. The monumental contexts have freed them from any suspicion that they might be decorative or merely doodles. Making them demands concentration and time, so they are likely to be inspired by a belief that they are worth making. It is difficult not to use the term 'religious' in understanding them, and to liken their impact to that of a cross to a Christian, but we tend to separate religious and secular in a way that might have been incomprehensible to prehistoric people. The motifs socialise and underline the importance of some places in the landscape, they may mark places where important events took place, act as waymarkers along important routes for animals, wild and tame. Where they cluster, they may mark important seasonal meeting places. They also mark stream sources in a few cases. Some decorated outcrops are places that attract the building of cairns, as places already revered for whatever reason.

How they originated and what they might mean are even more difficult questions to answer. Some people have looked at legend and folklore attached to some of the sites to explain them, but although it is possible that some residual significance may be attached to places, legends can be very recent and have nothing to do with prehistoric art, for how can we prove such things? People use sites according to the culture of the day. The symbolism is clearly very potent and extensively used, and the predominance of circles, occasional spirals and enclosures links the idea of the cup-and-ring to circular monuments. We do have a connection; the Neolithic view of the universe concentrated on the circle. Why? Could it be that the heavens themselves displayed the pattern for the idea? The shape of sun and moon are obvious as a source. The movement through the heavens is cyclic. The stars, to those without telescopes, may appear as holes in space. Add to that such things in nature as tree rings, the ripples of a stone dropped in water, parts of the human body that are curved or circular: eyes, breasts, buttocks, testicles, belly, the head itself. We can only speculate, but we can note that when prehistoric people made images of people they sometimes emphasised what they associated with fertility to the exclusion of less important characteristics.

When I began work on rock-art, I had some associations in my mind with what I saw on the rocks and their locations to the extent that I put this experience into a poem.

The Sculptured Rocks
In this design you petrified the language of your soul–
Your own symbolic logic;
Linked a little world with universe,
Arrested time with space.
You saw the cycle of your birth and death with clarity
As sun and moon spun round,
As buds burst into leaves and fell upon the nourished ground.
A rhythmic pulse beat out like water flow,
Rippled from your centre to the stars.
The living rocks bear traces of belief,
Knowing all you used to know.
The curlew cry spills out
A plaintive, bubbling message to the moors
Above the desecrated graves and broken stones
As it has always done.
Its curved beak swings down from the sun
To execute parabolas in heather-scented air,
Or sink in silence to an unresponsive earth.

Whatever delight I had from experiencing rock-art in this way, I have avoided saying anything that cannot be proved, for there is a gap between evidence and imaginative experience, poetry being one truth and logic another.

There is a theory of origin that has grown in popularity because it has been so apparently well-researched and articulated: that these images spring from our subconscious minds and are present in all people, ready to be brought to the surface. Dream-states, in which the conscious mind is relaxed, can produce images. Migraine can produce wavy lines, when reality will not keep still. Current research, brought together notably by Professor Lewis-Williams, states that:

> We need to examine human consciousness, not just in the alert, problem-solving state that we cultivate today, but also in the more mysterious states that, in some circumstances, become the essence of religion.

Experiences of altered consciousness are like those experienced by Coleridge in *Kubla Khan*, a trance-like state where images reach from the mind in sleep:

> Weave a circle round him thrice
> And close his eyes with holy dread
> For he on honey dew hath fed
> And drunk the milk of paradise.

So many of us are familiar with this, as it is well anthologised, was taught in schools, and famous too because the Person from Porlock interrupted Coleridge's recalling the dream in full. We also know that Coleridge took drugs, allowing him this altered consciousness. Lewis-Williams' interest in the neurological functioning of the brain, informed by research, has concluded that some images are common to all people at all times, independent of their culture. Our culture is not irrelevant, for what we inherit and experience allowed Coleridge to write a unique poem, so we have to look for the common, primitive images, which turn out to be some of the repertoire of rock-art not only in Britain but all over the world and at all times. We may be influenced by images of which we may not be aware. This suggests that such images are not taken from the natural world, but are locked into our brains from the time we are conceived. It provides a convincing thesis to explain why these images are universal, so that we do not have to look around for explanations of human contact across time and vast distances, for we know such things to be impossible (except for those who are wont to attribute them to beings from outer space).

I have found *Inside the Neolithic Mind* (Lewis-Williams 2005) interesting as a partly persuasive thesis to follow up his views on consciousness from

Palaeolithic to Neolithic, but many ask whether all religions stem from trance-like experiences because the brain has images already buried there, and that only a kind of priesthood or elite had access to these images. Priesthoods are not difficult to visualise, but when people begin to argue that British open-air rock-art, for example, is the result of some kind of shamanic activity, I do not know what evidence I am looking for. It is easier to envisage an elite deciding on the use of passage-graves and their art, or of a 'priesthood' conducting ceremonies or worshiping in a stone circle or henge, but this is an assumption made from our extensive knowledge of history and the premise that politics is a process whereby an elite is established and maintained, and this can be through all sorts of ways such as holding the food supplies and the means of production. Religion, as we all know to our cost, is another form of power that can be uncaring and ruthless. We have to go no further than the threat of fundamentalism, be it Crusades or a Fatwah.

We are all aware of 'themes' that are universal in rock-art, such as circles, spirals, serpent-shapes, chevrons, parallel and crossed lines, for they appear in primitive art all over the world. This has wrongly led some people to conclude that there has been communication between them, which is impossible. It is rational to understand that images which appear all over the world are common to all minds. Aboriginal concentric circles are like those in prehistoric Britain; they spring from the same desire to add circle to circle. I have observed that although many images produced by young children such as a sun symbol are taught by adults, this does not mean that all circles with lines radiating from them represent the sun, as some rock-art writers suppose. Others produced by children, such as human figures with long arms and legs and short bodies are explained by the child's view of adults from below.

Why circles? These are sometimes perceived as images of eternity, like the common image of a snake swallowing its own tail on eighteenth- and nineteenth-century gravestones, but we cannot assume that this is what they meant to everyone. Continuity, exclusion or inclusion may be some of their meanings. Often they are penetrated by a groove from a central cup; is this related to monuments that have an entrance or to the entrance into a round house? Were people so convinced of the 'magic' of the circle that they all wanted to build a Castlerigg or Stonehenge? Were they told to do so by elites, especially priestly elites? Did they do so voluntarily and with enthusiasm, or were they scared out of their wits about what would happen if they didn't conform? Who decided which symbols and motifs should be used, and where?

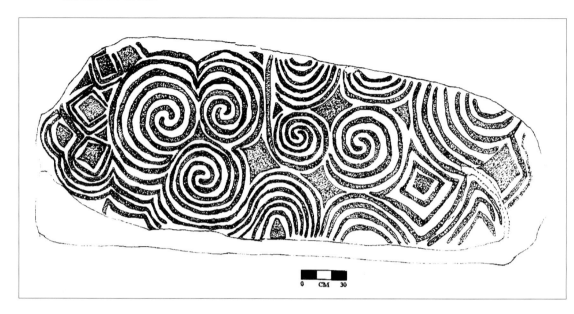

115 Newgrange stone at the entrance to the passage-grave

PASSAGE–GRAVE IMAGERY

It is in these darkened tombs that we find the strongest indication of the deliberate placing of linear and spiral images; elsewhere the vast majority are cups-and-rings, although these too are still present in the graves, sometimes hidden on the backs of stones or in other places where they cannot be seen. Here there is a repertoire of motifs that is as different from the run of the mill motifs as baroque/rococo architecture is from earlier architecture in the modern world, with a flowing exuberance incorporating spirals, triangles, lozenges, serpentine forms and crossed lines. These appear at the entrances to the passages, on lintels, kerbs and decorate large ceremonial basins. These cave-like structures bring us closer to the dead: quite different from the impact of open-air art. Passage-grave images, though specialised in their use, are not unique. Both the common open-air images and the tomb images are sometimes very skilfully contrived, with aesthetically pleasing results. In both tomb and cairn burials they can be present on the kerbstones, but the sheer size of the passage-graves, the huge decorated kerb slabs and the flat-top of Newgrange, where ceremonies might have taken place under the sun or stars, makes a big difference to how we see them. There may have been a dance or movement around the outsides of both kinds of mound as part of the ritual there, and in both the kinds of people allowed either to go into the passage and chambers or to prepare the cist burial in a round barrow might have been restricted to those most concerned, such as the nearest in kin or those at the top of the power structure. Although the cairn burials were sealed by the addition of cobbles or earth and stone, and any additions made by taking out some from the top and inserting another, the passage-graves may have been reopened periodically many times before finally sealing off the entrance. In some, the corbelled chamber suggests a movement to the heavens, like an ascension. Places like these, conceived and built by people, say as much by their architecture as the carved images in a way similar to that of a church, with its cruciform plan and the painted and other images inside the building. Progression of movement through both buildings must have been dictated by tradition; one has to think only of the easterly placing of the altar or the Stations of the Cross, or the restricted areas within the Sanctuary to see these parallels. In Maltese megalithic 'temples' and in the underground complexes like the Hypogeum, there is a megalithic architecture based on entrances that welcome through an enclosing curved outer wall, then a passage with elliptical chambers leading from it, usually in a clover-leaf pattern. The Hypogeum has its eerie sounding-box contrived from the underground stone. Painted in red on the ceiling of the Hypogeum and on the megaliths of Ggantija on Gozo are spirals and vine-like tendrils. Other motifs are drilled holes. It was in fact these temples that aroused my interest later in British rock-art when I worked and lived there. The placing of images, whether it is in buildings or in the open, always seems to be of great significance, part of which we may understand.

Hunches have no place in this understanding, for rock-art demands meticulous attention to details of kind and place before one theorises. The danger of jumping to rash and ill-informed conclusions is no better seen than in the theory handed out to the media after the discovery of the Fylingdales (NYM) inward-facing kerb slabs, one of which was declared the oldest rock-map in the world!

There is always room for individuality, even within the manipulation of a limited number of symbols. If you look at what the young people at Greenfield Community School produced in their response to seeing prehistoric rock-art without having seen any before, it is not hard to understand why so many of their works were different (see chapter 10).

THE DEAD IN TOMBS

The way people disposed of the dead suggests a ritual and a sense of continuity in a spirit world after death. Some Irish passage-graves point in no uncertain terms to the use of symbols and motifs in profusion. Although the kerbstones surrounding the great mounds carry simple and complex decoration, it is the interior, reached through passages, where a special and awesome place is constructed. Newgrange may have had some of the feeling taken out of it by being made presentable for an enquiring and eager public, but it is still a powerful experience. More so for me was a visit to the Loughcrew sites where there was no electric light and only 'darkness visible' in a passage-grave where I found myself surrounded by a remarkable array of symbols woven into designs. It was, quite frankly, frightening. Many have the same reaction to the restored mound of Maes Howe on Orkney. Having to crouch along a narrow, low tunnel to reach the main chamber is a preparation for this underworld experience.

The Irish passage-graves have decoration that seems so profuse that, compared with what we meet in the open-air, it seems over the top! It's like taking the Christian cross and covering it with jewels and multiple decorations compared with the simple wayside crosses on a pilgrim route. The passage-graves of the Boyne valley are the strongest statement in Britain of the power of place and symbol in prehistoric times. There is also a great sense of continuity there.

Seamus Heaney, for example, in his poem *Funeral Rites*, takes the site at Newgrange as a place where all human feeling and thought about the dead can be focused in a ritual now as in the past.

Buried motifs pose all sorts of questions. Are such motifs specially developed from simpler ones because their function becomes more important? The sense of place that we have when we visit these graves and ritual centres is dependent not only on the constructions themselves but also on their settings.

Of course the next question about graves and monuments is why they are not all decorated with cup-and-ring motifs and spirals. A few cups-and-rings have appeared in the south of England, but they are almost negligible. Were these motifs common on materials such as wood and cloth? Were they painted or tattooed on human skin? We do not know. Why were so few burials chosen to incorporate rock-art? Is this because the archaeological record is so patchy rather than its being a true picture of distribution? Why do Stonehenge and Kilmartin have the only axe motifs?

At least there is a period of use to be deduced when art is found in burial and monumental contexts. We can attribute it to a broad timescale from about 3000–2000 BC, with an overlap at either end. We can surmise that it had something to do with how monuments were used and how the dead were buried, but most British rock-art is in the landscape, so what purpose did the motifs serve there?

There is a difference between the motifs found in passage-graves and those in the open. Whereas the latter sit on outcrop and earthfast stones, the former are cut from rock, shaped and ordered to fit tomb design, enhanced by the exuberance of the decoration. Art used in later mounds in different areas from these giants has only limited cups and cups-and-rings incorporated. These tombs

116 Loughcrew passage-grave entrance

have a different function in cave-like ritual from landscape art, which is much more widespread and, presumably, accessible.

There is a difference in the form of the motifs. Patterns of lozenge-shapes, spirals, zigzags and wavy lines are also present on pottery. There is an early pottery style called Grooved Ware spread all over Britain that shares some of these motifs, and this is associated with open-air 'ritual' sites around passage-graves and henges. Style, however, is only one strand in the reasons for the difference between passage-grave and open-air art. If we were to choose to go by design alone, we may find linear designs and lozenge-shapes on Food Vessels, Beakers and urns, but as these vessels are from *c.*2000 BC and passage-graves are hundreds of years earlier, this shows the dangers of making comparisons. And, of course, this pottery exists widely where there is no rock-art. I can believe that locked up inside our brain or nerve centres are basic images common to all people, and that what we see on the rocks may have stemmed from some release, for how else can we account for the universal use of symbols such as cups, concentric rings, spirals, zigzags, lozenge-shapes? To see that a panel of rock-art in California could be equally at home in Scotland or Galicia points to some common inspiration not shared by transporting it over the sea at a given time. People do not have to meet in Britain to decide to put spirals on cliffs in Northumberland or on

Temple Wood (K), or to put rosettes on rock overlooking the sea at Ormaig (K) or on outcrop in Northumberland.

ROCK–ART IN THE OPEN–AIR; DISTRIBUTION IN THE LANDSCAPE

Although there seems to be a stronger link establishing the period of use and possible reasons for use in burials and monuments, the logic for its distribution in the landscape is clearer than many have supposed. We now have thousands of marked rocks recorded and an analysis of where they are found should help us to understand why they were put there and nowhere else. Hundreds have been destroyed, but there should be sufficient data to make some intelligent suggestions.

We observe something in the landscape, something revealed, and we ask questions about it. We form a theory, but the next step is to work hard at finding what brought us to that theory in the first place. It is a leap of imagination that must be traced back to our minds and our experience. We have to find a method to assess the value of our interpretations; this needs discipline.

The rocks are 'signs', places in the landscape that gave information, and would have had meanings for the people there. That applies to any rock-art area in Britain, for just by walking the routes from one panel to another gives a sense of markers being offered, without our being able to understand what those particular symbols mean. Whereas archaeology relies on such things as settlements and artefacts for an understanding of people, a different approach is needed here because the element of mobility has to be taken into account. People whose lives depend entirely or partially on moving around the landscape cannot afford to clash with other groups, and need to define their areas of special interest. Perhaps marking the rocks with their signs would do this. The more dependent people were on farming in one place, with defined fields for crops and pasture, and for living in, the less mobile their lives, although they would still need to pasture animals outside the settlement and to hunt. These hunting and pasture areas, outside the most fertile arable lands, would have been in what we call 'marginal' land, not the best for arable farming, but still rich in food. In Northumberland, around the fertile Milfield plain, where the ritual monuments lie and where the best arable land is, are sandstone scarps cut into areas by streams and by the River Till. The same marginal areas also include most burial cairns, mostly of the Late Neolithic/Early Bronze Age type. If rock-art defines areas of grazing for one group, then such areas may be crossed or be linked by trails, as beasts do not pasture in one spot. Some archaeologists believe that the decline in use of rock motifs was the result of a decline in the mobility of prehistoric peoples, and this has been used for suggesting a very early date for rock-art: more settled farming/less need to mark the rocks as mobility decreased. I see no reason why mobile grazing should decline because of settled farming; hunting and pasture continued to be essential to life, especially as population increased and more food was always needed. Mainstream archaeology missed out something significant by not seeing mobility as important, and instead of seeing rock-art as 'a medium for wider study of prehistoric society and its occupation of the landscape' (Bradley) they have treated rock-art in the same way as portable artefacts.

What was rock-art advertising? What information was it giving? Whatever answers may come from this, one may be sure that we have no means of knowing precisely what it meant. As it was used over such a considerable period of time, it is even unlikely the people who made the motifs were aware of how the whole process began. That does not mean that people went through some meaningless and outdated ritual when they made the marks. They must have known that what they were doing was important and of great significance. We use words without thinking about how they came into being or of what they are composed. We use symbols in everyday life without thinking about why they were chosen to mean what they mean. The fact that the motifs are abstract does not help us to understand them; such motifs may hold many meanings for the people who made and understood them, like 'layers of meaning' in poetry. Not only that, but also the meaning of the images may have changed over time.

If we accept that whatever we do we may not be able to 'crack the code' that leaves us with the more profitable task of trying to find a logic to their distribution in the landscape. There is plenty of data that enables us to make distribution maps. We can place sites and single marked rocks precisely on a map, draw diagrams to show their height above sea level, find out what kind of rock they are pecked on and whether they are related in their distribution to various types of soil. Do clusters of marked rocks in a limited area mean that people congregated there at special times? One of the things that has resulted from my own extensive fieldwork and that of my friends is an instinct about where to look for new rock-art, for through this we have discovered many new sites. This 'hunch' can hardly be blind instinct, for we have learnt about places, about rock types, about topography. It is as if somewhere in our brains we are using the same logic as prehistoric people in deciding where rock-art might or ought to be.

One starting point in the search for new marked rocks is in areas where they already have been found. It is rather like finding one flint flake in a ploughed field; it directs attention to the possibility or probability of finding more. When Reading students were working with Richard Bradley and me on rock-art, they were specifically asked not to look for new sites. Some people have an uncanny instinct for finding totally new ones. Why? Diligence and interest, of course, and prior knowledge – but some other sense seems to be at work. Very high places are out, and intensively ploughed areas are not usually forthcoming, but the marginal intermediate higher ground is where we find them. Within an established rock-art area, the surprises and delights of discovery are our reward. In Northumberland one of the most spectacular recent finds was on the floor of a rock-shelter at Ketley Crag. The shelter was in a minor Fell Sandstone scarp that fell away to a stream valley. The most that it could have afforded was a temporary small shelter for two or three people, huddled together, yet the floor has some of the most skilful use of the natural floor as a base for intricate rock-art as any we have ever encountered. The significance of the place could not have been just as a shelter, for other rock overhangs would have proved more effective. Can we really say why it was singled out? There is other rock-art on the higher ground above it, some of very high quality. The view from the overhang is so widespread and spectacular – over the valley to the distant Cheviot Hills – that its location as a commanding spot must have been one reason for its choice. Could other rocks along the same outcrop have been used? Probably yes, so we may have to acknowledge that other factors were at work in making a choice, and the level of artistry made it even more special. As a meeting place for special occasions it might not have been very suitable as it is on a rather awkward slope. There is a much more suitable dome of rock above it, with rock-art that is good, but not as impressive as this.

We can expect patterns to emerge now, but must be prepared for something to challenge our expectations. However, we can make some generalisations about where people placed their motifs.

In Ireland, Kilmartin, Tayside, Yorkshire, Galloway, County Durham and part of Northumberland the bulk of rock-art occupies high places that overlook lower ground, bordering and overlooking a loch, surrounding and overlooking a long, flat valley, and forming an area of low hills around a flat plain, for example. The pattern is also one that follows rivers and stream courses. Rivers and streams give access to the land, and provide essential water for animals. Rock-art also marks the actual sources of streams and overlooks river estuaries. These examples alone show how rock-art 'socialises' landscapes, imprinting human signs at specific places. There were already many places that would allow travellers, distant or local, to know where they were in their journey; cliffs, large boulders, certain trees would be familiar because they are outstanding. Rock-art is lower key; it takes an existing rock surface, studies its form, and begins to use natural indentations, cracks and the shape of the rock itself to produce a design based on simple symbols. In a way this then enhances the landscape, it humanises it in what could have appeared as a dangerous wilderness; it would have been reassuring.

I find that this is my reaction when I find a new decorated panel. It is familiar, yet different, for every rock is different. Beyond the excitement of making a new discovery, it generates a warmth of familiarity for me. It increases my sense of wonder, links me with a past that I only sense in part. If the area itself were unknown to me, as Tayside used to be, until quite recently, the very existence of rock-art made me feel at home; so much so that I am convinced that prehistoric people visiting that area would have felt the same reassurance. It does not matter how long ago the decoration was made – hundreds, thousands of years ago; it spoke of continuity and reinforced a common identity. People were leaving behind something of themselves, and this was intentionally permanent when rocks are worked on with mallet and pick. We who find them record, preserve and try to place them in a context, a sequence. We follow a gut reaction, we attempt to devise a method to understand it; we look beyond our own countries to others where rock-art appears to see what can be learnt there. We ask: What made them do it? Who in society made them – a selected few, perhaps?

A very difficult question that I ask is: As markings on outcrop rock would soon be covered over by vegetation unless someone kept it clear, did people act as caretakers?

The problem of arranging rock-art panels according to their position in the landscape is that, no matter what categories of place are decided, some panels are going to be in more than one category. The general distribution of rock-art is largely centred on intermediate high places overlooking valleys. It does not appear on the highest ground, and rarely occupies valley floors.

The following areas of placement are a guide:

There are sites overlooking or close to the sea.
Some rocks are at high places dominating or marking routeways to and from the sea.
There are other routeway sites at high places.
There are decorated rocks at stream sources.
Most sites overlook valleys from slopes.
Rarely, decorated outcrop may be on a valley floor.
Many sites are related to burials and monuments.

Other sites include portables, sometimes built into other old and new structures. We have discovered many more sites in the past 10 years, yet questions about the origin of the symbols and motifs, on why they are where they are, will continue to concern people for many years to come.

As we have seen, there is intense interest today in the state of mind of people who carved rocks in prehistoric times. There is a particularly intriguing question about why on the continent there are so many picture images whereas in Britain we have non-figurative images. The figurative images, whether they be in caves or later depictions hammered onto rock surfaces, have always attracted more attention, because people think they know where they are with them. Almost all rock-art in monuments, in burials and in the landscape of Britain is non-figurative. In cup-and-ring art, there are many variations such as arcs, rectangles, grids and squares that give variety that can be attributed to an individual seeing it in a different way. The end result is non-representational art. All these variations cannot be demonstrated to have come from nature. We might see ripple marks in pools, zigzag skylines of hills and trees, the annual rings of a fallen tree, vulvas, breasts or whatever as sources for these images, but where is the evidence that this is what they are?

The distribution of similar motifs over Britain is hardly surprising when seen against the similarity in styles of pottery, artefacts, house construction, and farming methods, even though the rock-art and these other prehistoric phenomena do not necessarily coincide. Neither is it surprising that rock-art in Galicia is so much like that in Britain, for the sea was obviously not an insuperable barrier. What is difficult to account for is the virtual absence of rock-art in the south of England. It may have taken a more perishable form, and may have been inhibited by a lack of suitable rock surfaces, but it is still odd. Against that we must take into account that it was by no means widespread in northern Britain. It is scattered thinly in parts, and there are more concentrated patches in other areas. It does occur in burials, but why should Ireland house the greatest passage-graves with their art?

For those who want to see the art in those tombs as being inspired by shamans under the influence of drugs, it would be wise for them to listen to George Eogan, the man who has excavated them for years and who knows them all intimately. When he was interviewed for *Current Archaeology* (October 2003) by Andrew Selkirk with the question 'Do you believe in these current ideas about it being inspired by shamans under the influence of drugs': A slight pause. 'No' he said abruptly, and seemed to want to change the subject.

The issue remains open, and is likely to do so no matter how far the theory applies to other cultures at others times. We do not have any direct evidence of the presence of shamans or of their influence on rock-art in Britain. But we do know that people have shared basic images all over the world, and that shamanism and that fact are not interdependent.

There is always a danger in interpretation that people go for the explanation that they would like most to believe in, without checking carefully the scientific evidence for it. The media particularly choose the dramatic, eye-catching, and often simplistic, and we see, particularly on television, masses of waffle covering very little. We see pretty faces lit up by computer screens, people travelling rapidly through countries on trains or in cars, accompanied by music that drowns out what is being said. Scientists who have been consulted by the programme-makers are often horrified with the results and try to distance themselves from what has been produced. One big problem is that few people understand science, and too readily believe what they are being told. If the theory draws upon only the evidence that supports the theory and does not emerge from the evidence, this is dishonest and wrong, and sadly we see far too much of this. That is why so many theories presented to the general public have such a short shelf-life, and this should warn us not to follow unthinkingly whatever is current. In all this scientists and archaeologists have a great responsibility, and must not compromise their integrity for momentary fame and money. Archaeologists are seldom scientists, although many like to put on that mantle.

Those of us who have researched rock-art in Britain the most deeply, may feel privileged. I do. All history is shadowy, as we only know in part, but this is particularly shrouded. We have had to steer through the crankiness of some totally unsupported theories, separate fact from mythology, face the frustration and challenge of wanting to know more. We may even feel that in a sense we did not choose the subject, but that it chose us, when there might have been some other aspect of learning rather safer to pursue.

In return for my efforts I have explored landscapes that I might not have otherwise seen, been forced into places difficult of access, physically demanding, and through them discovering an extraordinary variety and beauty, when rain drenches rocks and the sun breaks through to reveal motifs of extraordinary richness. The art is only one part of a larger experience that the land has to offer. There is a sense of people having lived there, using it to survive, cursing it at times, loving it, moving away from it when it became exhausted, burying their dead there, carrying within their genes a whole history of change. Through them I have met other people that I might not have met, shared thoughts and ideas with strangers here and abroad, been reminded that the whole point of history is that it is about people and relationships. And I am perhaps fitter than I would have been without my archaeological fieldwork. I am also grateful that this has not been my job, my means of earning a living, with the pressure of the need to publish or to prove myself in one field. I can choose to do this work or not to do anything. Like the ancient people whose lives have briefly touched mine, I try to come to terms with what I have inherited and to understand a little more about what links all human beings.

9

Recording, conservation and display

RECORDING

Since the study of rock-art became part of mainstream archaeology, our approach to it has changed. Whereas recording in the past was haphazard and depended on the time given to it and skill of individuals, it has become an activity which involves many people and institutions, and many disciplines. Recording the exact location of rock-art in the landscape is no longer a problem, for the use of GPS has solved that. What is still being debated is the best way to record a decorated surface accurately.

When the English Heritage Rock Art Pilot Project (RAPP) was set up and running in 1999, one priority of the survey was to find out exactly how much was known already. There are many sources, including books and papers, and many regions have a Sites and Monuments Record (SMR) of what is on their patch. However, it soon became clear that the standard of recording was variable, and that there was a need to produce an agreed common standard.

Rock-art has to be drawn and photographed. That sounds straight-forward, but isn't. A glance at many reports will show that some drawings are free-hand and approximate. There is little attempt to show the natural structure of a rock surface, with its cracks and indentations; drawings in thick or thin black lines take no account of the relationships between one motif and another. For example, some motifs are fainter than others, and there are some traces of superimposition of symbols and motifs. No attempt, even in modernity, has been made to find a way of recording the varied depths of cups and grooves. Professor John Coles, who has done extensive work developing recording systems in Scandinavia, writes: 'I suggest that the days of simple black and white illustration, devoid of structure and variation, should now be drawn to a conclusion'. He also suggests that any system should include 'the depth of the carvings' (Coles 2003).

As a principle, a technique that has no direct contact with a rock surface is best. Thus photogrammetry and laser scanning are favoured. The problem at the moment of recording all rock surfaces in this manner is that it is expensive and requires the portability of some equipment. It is ironic that many who have turned up their noses at the wax-rubbing method of recording on a one-off basis have not thought to question the presence of animals in the fields, acid rain, and harmful vegetation growth, people walking over the surfaces or even the continuous exposure of rock surfaces as being infinitely dangerous to a fragile heritage. The purpose of rubbing, carried out by experts, is purely as a basis for an accurate drawing. Had I not used this technique myself, you would not be seeing my accurate drawings in this book, and those that I have recorded number in the hundreds. Realistically, one cannot cart much equipment around the moorland to reach remote areas where there is rock-art, and when a new panel is found, the priority has to be to record it as quickly and accurately as possible. Now that that work has been done, it is fine to consider re-recording the most accessible to check standards of accuracy.

Wax-rubbing in which black wax is rubbed on the surface of thin, strong newsprint, is a method that I have used to great effect, but this is an acquired skill; without plenty of practice and patience this can give subjective results. Many systems of recording suffer from the operator making assumptions about the way the pattern is developing, and may be wrong. Even with the most careful rubbing on paper over a clean surface, the results must be checked against photographs taken in strong, oblique light, preferably not at one time or season only.

If the rubbings, which are a primary source of information, are to be stored, there may be a problem with the type of paper used. Many advocate acid-free paper, but this is expensive. The whole purpose is not to produce decorative wall-coverings but to provide a basis for an accurate drawing. In most cases this is perfectly possible, but as the surface of a rock undulates and dips, there is bound to be a distortion of area when it is reduced to a flat surface.

I have on occasions produced a few versions of the same markings on the same rock over a period of time, each an improvement on the last. That's fine; one is fallible, and one has to face the fact that one might not get the drawing exactly right the first time. There is always something, especially on a large, difficult surface, that one may have missed. If an alternative method gets rid of human error, fine.

The rubbing may be covered with a grid of 10cm squares so that the information can be transferred to graph paper, giving a scale of 1/10. Then the drawing is made, with further reference to photographs and to further visits to the site to check all details. Symbols have to be devised so that natural markings are distinguished from artificial. Wherever motifs are clearly spaced there is no problem; where and how motifs merge must be shown. This method of recording is not infallible, and may only be applied to Scheduled Ancient Monuments with express permission.

Another method is to cover the rock with a sheet of polythene and use a felt pen to draw the design. This sounds satisfactory, but is less objective than a rubbing. Motifs cannot be easily seen under plastic unless they have been filled in with some substance beforehand; this translates the pattern decided by the eye onto the tracing. Corrections can be made, however, to the final drawing in the light of good photographs and through selective rubbings of difficult areas. A glance at any report from anywhere in the world shows that there are many methods of drawing. Some use dark grooves against a white background; others have white grooves against a stippled or shaded background. Some put in a sharp edge to cups-and-rings; others a fuzzy edge. There is as yet no agreed single method. The key question is: what detailed information is a drawing expected to give?

Even when drawings are good, they still need to be complemented by good photographs. Black and white is an excellent medium, and those taken years ago outlive colour prints. Today's technology allows colour prints to be turned into black and white, and colour itself can be enhanced and adjusted. Digital images are particularly useful in close-ups and do not require a great deal of light, although oblique sunlight shows details better. There is a standard scale now accepted, produced by IFRAO, that shows not only centimetres but colours. In the past we have all been in the field when, for various reasons, an acceptable scale has not been available, and coins, walking sticks, pencils, spectacles, buckets, combs and anything handy have been used as scale. In time these items may come to date the photographs for which they provided scales! Information that accompanies the drawings and photography must include details of the area and its recorded archaeology. The type of rock must be noted too, and the presence of growths on the rock such as lichens – all of which help when establishing the rock's 'history'.

A 360-degree photographic image around a rock is desirable, and there are special lenses for this.

Each generation of recorders builds upon another; this must be a genuine improvement, and not copying. We see too many mistakes and oversights repeated in drawings.

Recording may begin with known sites, which already may indicate that there are others in the area. This is where teams, rather like those employed in traditional field-walking, can be effective. If a rock is showing some symbols and the rest are covered over, there has to be a policy about how to proceed. As rock-art tends to occur in clusters, it 'runs out', and then the search has to move wider. Here, another sense comes into play: knowing where rock-art is located makes it possible to search areas where one anticipates it to be. My friends and I find new areas and sites in this way. Perhaps we are using the same logic as the people who made the motifs.

Once all the motifs on rocks are recorded, one has to consider how they can be analysed; researchers draw up a vocabulary ranging from the basic symbol, a cup, to all kinds of complex designs that form a panel. Recordings should always show relationships between them, as it is of interest to know how a design was conceived. For example, if a cup, with a groove leading from it, lies at the centre of concentric rings, did the rings stop at the groove because it was already there, or does the groove cut rings that were made first?

There is a tendency to give precedence to 'exotic' motifs such as spirals, rosettes and rectangles, but we must remember that the vast majority are cups-and-rings. The addition of multiple concentric circles up to 10 in number produces a dramatic effect, yet this is but a variation on a simple theme.

Such a limited range of symbols is bound to result in an individual producing a design that he or she has not seen before, and this can happen in areas miles away from one another by chance.

All rock-art recording must give an account of its context. In the future more areas around rock panels should be scanned and excavated; only a few have received this treatment so far.

The most thorough and effective system of collating data in the UK has been developed at Newcastle University. This is not the place to examine it in detail, but it meets all the criteria of the precision that is required (Mazel 2003, ongoing). The data is available in such a way that it can be cross-referenced by types, parishes, accessibility, the history of the rocks and even the meaning of the place names where they are to be found, for example. It is so successful that in its first year it had 5.8 million 'hits'. That means that there is a great deal of interest and sharing of information all over the world of the Northumberland Archive. It is able to accommodate all regions of Britain in a coherent, universal system, although its scope at the time of writing is confined to Northumberland.

As the Newcastle Museum of Antiquities has a large hidden cache of prehistoric marked rocks, one aim is to extend museum and other facilities to encourage everyone to use the information. That said, an English Heritage Report (2000) states that:

> It would be better to achieve complete coverage at a standard level (that later could be enhanced if resources became available) rather than attain partial cover at a deluxe level in some areas and nothing at all in others.

That would be all very well, but as little has happened to achieve this since the report was written, it is better to support the real work being done and build on that.

To make up for lost time, English Heritage has funded a Northumberland and Durham project led by Dr Tertia Barnett to train volunteers to take part in rock-art research and to re-record the hundreds of rocks already recorded. Other projects are going ahead all over Britain, encouraged by public funding, and all the resources made available should pay back in not only growing awareness of the importance of rock-art, but in discovery, leading to answers perhaps to some of our unanswered questions.

There is more international cooperation on methods of recording, as on other aspects of rock-art. In September 2005, a group of rock-art experts (including the author) from different countries was convened by UNESCO and the French National Museum, at Eyzies de Tayac, to prepare a policy that UNESCO could offer as a model to governments. As we were all researchers in the field, bringing to it a great deal of practical experience, as opposed to ivory-tower theory, we were very much in accord about priorities, so much so that any one delegate would have written a similar report. There are many other international bodies that represent countries, but this was a special gathering, carefully chosen for the varied experiences of its members, and the results should be out sometime soon.

THREATS TO ROCK-ART, CONSERVATION AND MANAGEMENT

The dangers to rock-art must be assessed. In Britain human intervention, particularly in the form of quarrying and farming has led to the destruction of many panels or to their defacement. A priority is to ensure that those we know about should be legally and scientifically protected. Another threat to decorated rocks is a natural one: that exposure opens up some rocks to the action of water, frost, acid rain and the growth of lichens. In the latter case we are still not sure what effect lichens have on rock-art. It seems logical that, if they grow on a rock surface, they are drawing out minerals to feed on. On the other hand, the cover that lichens and mosses provide may protect the rock from other kinds of erosion. There is a clear need for an objective study.

As rock-art has become so popular throughout the world to visitors, this popularity is both a blessing and a danger. That people wish to share a heritage is laudable, but some still wish to add their names and scrawls as a cheap sort of immortality. We see names, initials and dates chiselled into the rocks at such places as Ormaig. That this is not general in the Kilmartin area is partly due to making people aware of the importance and fragility of the motifs, and by satisfying their needs by providing controlled access. This is a management problem shared by all historical sites. In Scotland there is considerable work being done to assess and remedy any threats to decorated surfaces, not only on prehistoric sites but at all places where stonework, marked or not, is in danger. An important document on this, *Carved Stones: Historic Scotland's Approach*, set out the score in 2003.

Conservation and management go hand in hand. Monument status theoretically gives a rock legal protection, but in reality that does not protect it. I know of many rocks that have been removed, and have reported this. Protection involves making intelligent decisions on which panels are best displayed and which should be covered over. Is the action of weather eroding the marks? That sounds an easy question to answer, but it isn't, for the time of the year or day when markings are viewed makes them appear strong or faint. There has to be a more objective method.

How often are marked rocks visited by inspectors? Infrequently at present; never in some places. This is where a local involvement is important: people who care enough to visit ought to report anything worrying. It is more desirable to have regional groups made responsible rather than distant bureaucracy, and for these groups to form a larger network for the purposes of standardisation. Rock-art must get its fair share of the budget for such work; we pay for its protection out of our taxes. It is easy to overlook such a small part of our heritage when spending millions on upstanding architecture. Such an important part of our history, and such an intriguing mystery draws thousands to visit Kilmartin and similar sites every year, but too much may be left to chance. We need to publicise rock-art more, to make it more generally available, especially to children and schools. When people are directed to sites, the sites must be displayed to the highest standards of interpretation and good taste.

In the field it is important that rock-art should not be seen as something detached from the landscape as a whole. In this, Kilmartin is an ideal situation, as one views it alongside other prehistoric remains. A tour of the well-displayed panels takes in so much of the landscape around it and gives the visitor a strong sense of place. The trail can be extended. At the same time other demands on the landscape are evident: forestry, quarrying, arable and livestock farming. It is essential to get a balance between the needs of tourism and industry. It is hard for a farmer whose sheep are lambing to have to face a problem of uncontrolled visitors' dogs crossing the field. The lessons that we have learnt in Britain and continue to learn through selective excavation and site management may be shared with the rest of the world, and we can learn much from the experience of other countries. We must be uncompromising in reaching for the highest standards. The past deserves it and the future expects it of us.

What is left for us to see is what we can delight in. The places where rock-art occurs, often remote, needing effort to find, can be extraordinary in their beauty. There is a strong sense of place, of the past, of a mystery. The markings themselves, such an integral part of the landscape, can be profuse and varied or of incredible simplicity, where a single cup mark must have had powerful meaning. It is as important to our heritage as monuments that may well dwarf it and shout for our attention. Rock-art intrigues not only by its presence but also by its provocation. 'You do not and you cannot know everything, for all your searching', it seems to say, but it gently prods us to go on with the quest for knowledge.

10

The joy of discovery

In the spring of 2004 I was asked to assist with 'a journey of exploration into the past' called 'Written in Stone'. Young people from Greenfield Community School, Newton Aycliffe, were involved in a series of workshops, Lottery-funded, initiated by Creative Partnerships. With support from their excellent young art teachers and various specialists, the young people were put into situations where they could explore their environments and respond to them in their own way in various artistic media, including glass-making.

My role was to begin the exploration with them. After visiting the school and meeting them all, we were happy with one another. They were to spend a long week-end in Northumberland in a residential centre at Belford, and visit prehistoric rock-art sites. I asked them not to try to learn anything about the art in advance, but to respond to what they saw.

I chose Roughting Linn, the largest rock-art panel in England to start, but came to it via a magnificent little waterfall in a deep small gorge nearby, then over the curving ramparts of an enclosure to the rock itself. I wanted to begin with its setting; good weather ensured that we had the perfect start, for when we reached the panel there were strong shadows that threw the cups-and-rings into relief. This was their first encounter with art over 4000 years old, and they were enthralled.

The questions began, their reactions became vocal, and they responded directly to their own experiences. No one was there to tell them what they should think and the staff recorded some of these first impressions and developments of their ideas.

Examples follow:

The first time I saw them I thought that they were like explosions – I'm puzzled. They are almost symmetrical, but not quite perfect – like people, nobody is the same.

Left and below: 117, 118 Roughting Linn (N) waterfall and rock

Opposite: 119, 120, 121 Some responses to Roughting Linn in glass

122 Ketley Crag (N) rock-shelter with one of the young artists

123 Bamburgh beach (N): responses to rock-art

Bunches of circles on a rock in the middle of nowhere, it does not seem to make
   any sense. I had never really thought about art being in the middle of nowhere.
I would not want to find out why they are there; that is part of the beauty of
   them.
People could have put them there to mark territories.
Maybe they were a way of communicating.
They remind me of astrology/star signs; I am proper into my star sign.
Once we started talking more, we started to get more interested; before, I did not
   really think how they could have got there.
Nobody actually really knows what they are; it opens up possibilities.
I like the mystery of them.
You can make them what you want them to be.

I could spend a long time commenting on all these profound reactions!

The next day I exposed them to an open landscape with fantastic views across valleys to the Cheviot Hills, on top of a sandstone scarp at Chatton Park Hill, where there is some of the finest rock-art in the world. Sheets of decorated outcrop rock with multiple concentric circles, motifs on a rock at the centre of a prehistoric enclosure, and – most dramatically – the profusely-decorated floor of the Ketley Crag rockshelter. This is truly art, for the rock surface, with all its indentations and slopes had determined the design by an artist totally at one with his, her, or their medium.

This marvellous series of viewpoints occupied much of our time, but I was aware that young teenagers needed something different; so off we went to the beach at Bamburgh, where the sweep of pure sand is amazingly free of people. There, after the physical delight of such a beach, they all began to make motifs in the sand, guided by what they had seen, but improvising too, adding their own. One of the boys was put into a cist, made out of sand and decorated with symbols.

The evenings were for discussion, creation and information built on the experiences of the day. I took my three Tyne Tees TV programmes along for them to see, taken on different local sites. The teacher in charge invited a tutor in stained glass, and she talked about her work to prepare them for their own introduction to the art of glass-making at Sunderland.

After this I lost sight of them all for many weeks until they asked me to open their exhibition at the Museum of Antiquities, at Newcastle University. I was stunned by the quality of what they produced, especially as it was all such individually different work. The whole process of discovery was revealed too with all the aids of modern technology. It included an experience of practical archaeology at Bamburgh Castle, work in glass at Sunderland, the study of images

124 Glass spirals on display at the Newcastle Museum of Antiquities. *Sharon Simpson*

in their own town in the company of a University of Durham geographer, and the constant, intelligent support of their school.

Very few young people are likely to have such an opportunity, but with this level of resource and staffing, they have shown what can be done. It is a standard to be aimed at, and the principles on which the project was based are valid at any level of teaching. The work was moved from Newcastle, where it took its place among artefacts and sculpture of the past, back to a display at the school.

What characterised the work of these young people was their lack of preconception in their approach and the originality of what they produced. It does not always work like that for established artists. In September 1996 there was a theme on 'Northern Rock Art' at Durham Art Gallery, to which contemporary artists submitted work based on Prehistoric Carvings. At the same time there was one of the biggest collections of rock-art ever assembled, with boulders and slabs from as far north as Jedburgh and as far south as Dalton.

This made an interesting display, but some of the artists' work was really what they had already done, with some rock-art motifs added: not all was an organic response like that of the young people, although it made an interesting display of different approaches. Meanwhile jewellery with motifs, particularly spirals, appeals to the 'Celtic' tastes, and some local artists decorate pebbles with recorded patterns.

At Durham, Alnwick and Penrith, children have been encouraged to respond to the motifs in their own way, with interesting results. I was once contacted by a restaurant in the Midlands for permission to use one of my recorded drawings as the basis for wall decoration, and people abroad sometimes send me pictures of their creations.

Further back in time, I recall a group of American teachers who were on a short course with me at Alnwick Castle who became so interested in the art forms that they responded by creating their own interpretation on curtain materials, with concentric circles formed by string on nails driven into a board, and with beach flotsam which they formed into a cup-and-ring collage.

All this is not surprising, as it shows how we can respond in our own ways to these ancient, yet modern, images.

CONCLUSION

We weigh up the world in the balance of our own experience and, as we have seen, people are stimulated by images from the past to re-express them in their own way. However, the reader may wish to be left with something more objective and more 'certain' than this, so what follows is a summary of why circles in stone present a mystery to us, why they are where they are, and what they might mean.

There is a mystery because the rock motifs do not appear to draw on definite images taken from the natural world. They may remind us of something there, but we cannot say for sure what. It is difficult, even impossible, to enter the minds of those who lived thousands of years ago when we carry in our minds so much history and experience of our own.

The world in which rock-art was created was seen as largely 'circular', as all the major monuments testify. Stone and wooden circles and ditches focused not only scattered communities of farmers on a place in a wider landscape, but also focused shared beliefs. They appear as meeting places for all kinds of communal activities and rituals which were fundamental to their way of life. I use the term 'ritual' to mean acts which are repeated so often that they become formalised, as this is what circles in the landscape do. The ancestors dwelt there, perhaps; the sun, moon and stars pursued their courses above the monuments in a regular pattern. Their houses too were circular at this time, and, like them, the henges, and stone and wooden circles had essential and well-defined entrances. Being inside was different from observing the world from the outside; the focus of attention on the outside world was directed and not random.

The link between these monuments and the motifs hammered onto rocks, whatever may have been their function, was the circle, not only on outcrop and earthfast rocks, but on some of the monuments themselves. The cup remained the most basic of these circles. Their presence in some monuments emphasises their serious, deeply-held purpose. In the landscape, much of which was used not just for arable farming, but for pastoral and hunting purposes, the motifs are found at special places such as viewpoints, stream sources, and some of the most accessible routes across the landscape. The marked rocks do not often dominate the landscape, but are low-key, blending in with the natural landforms, usually near-horizontal, and would therefore be more difficult to locate than a cliff or prominent outcrop. One would have to know where to look for them, and perhaps keep the surfaces clear of vegetation that would soon obscure them. This complicates the issue even more when we remember that the time-span over which the marks were created may have been over a thousand years, and that however many we find, they still do not amount to many. Were some re-worked by successive generations? Were they all created in one region in a short time, added to or changed? If so, they were potent symbols for many generations using that landscape. Over such a long period, could their origins have been remembered, and did their meaning change?

Rock-art has many functions, marking places where people gather, perhaps to celebrate their regional identity, yet if they were to move away from their areas, they might find similar markings in other landscapes. Some may mark important events, such as a feat of heroism, a death, a humorous episode –who knows?

As we have seen, people can seize upon imagery and develop it to make it their own contribution to art. As the symbols and motifs used are universal, the creation of a design is a result of someone manipulating the images individually, although it is likely that some people, although miles apart, hit upon the same idea, even as far apart as another corner of the world, for the images used in Britain are present everywhere, common to many minds, but perhaps meaning different things; rock-art spans not only many centuries but also many parts of the world.

We have learnt much more about British rock-art since the antiquarians of the nineteenth century began to be interested, making progress in discovering many new sites and learning different ways of recording, but we are still asking the questions that they asked, and more. The future will have to concentrate on answering questions by choosing selective sites for survey and excavation that may answer research questions, both in the open-air and in monuments. Hand in hand with that must be the development of a coherent policy of preserving and displaying the rock-art that we have, making it known to more people so that they too can share the challenge and the pleasure of an important part of world history.

11

Bibliography

Books and papers listed below will contain guides to additional sources of information.

Books

Bahn, P. (Ed.) 1991. *Rock Art and Prehistory* (Oxford, Oxbow)

Bahn, P. 1998. *The Cambridge Illustrated History of Prehistoric Art* (Cambridge UP)

Bahn, P. and Rosenfeld, A. (Eds) 1988. *Rock art and prehistory – papers presented to symposium G of the AURA Congress, Darwin* (Oxbow Monograph No 10)

Beckensall, S. and Laurie, T. 1998. *Prehistoric Rock Art of County Durham, Swaledale and Wensleydale* (County Durham Books, Durham County Council)

Beckensall, S. 1999. *British Prehistoric Rock Art* (Tempus)

Beckensall, S. 2001a. *Northumberland: the Power of Place* (Tempus)

Beckensall, S. 2001b. *Prehistoric Rock Art in Northumberland* (Tempus)

Beckensall, S. 2002a. *Prehistoric Rock Art in Cumbria* (Tempus)

Beckensall, S. 2002b. *British Prehistoric Rock Art* (Tempus)

Beckensall, S. 2003. *Prehistoric Northumberland* (Tempus)

Beckensall, S. 2005. *The Prehistoric Rock Art of Kilmartin* (Kilmartin House Trust)

Beckensall, S. 2006. *Placenames and Fieldnames of Northumberland* (Tempus)

Boughey, K.J.S. and Vickerman, E.A. 2003. *Prehistoric Rock Art of the West Riding* (Yorkshire Archaeology 9, West Yorkshire Archaeology Service)

Bradley, R. 1993. *Altering the Earth* (Edinburgh)

Bradley, R. 1997. *Rock Art and the Prehistory of Atlantic Europe* (Routledge)

Bradley, R. 1998. *The Significance of Monuments* (Routledge)

Bradley, R. 2000. *The Good Stones* (SAS. Monograph Series 17)

Bradley, R. 2005. *The Moon and the Bonfire* (SAS Edinburgh)

Brown, P. and Chappell, G. 2005. *Prehistoric Rock Art of North Yorkshire* (Tempus)

Burl, A. 1979. *The Stone Circles of the British Isles* (Yale)

Burl, A. 1988. *Prehistoric Stone Circles* (Shire Publications Ltd)

Chippindale, C. and Tacon, S.C. (Eds) 1998. *The Archaeology of Rock-Art* (Cambridge)

Cooney, G. 2000. *Landscapes of Neolithic Ireland* (Routledge)

Coles, J. 2005. *Shadows of a Northern Past* (Oxbow)

English Heritage 2000. *Rock Art Pilot Project Proposals* (Limited circulation)

Eogan, G. 1986. *Knowth and the Passage Tombs of Ireland* (London: Thames and Hudson)

Eogan, G. 1984/1997. *Excavations at Knowth Vols. 1 and 2* (Royal Irish Academy)

Hadingham, E. 1974. *Ancient Carvings in Britain: A Mystery* (London)

Harding, J. 2003. *Henge Monuments of the British Isles* (Tempus)

Helvenston, A. and Bahn, P. 2005. *Waking the Trance-Fixed* (Wasteland Press, Louisville, USA)

Ilkley Archaeological Group. 1986. *The Carved Rocks on Rombalds Moor* (Wakefield)

Lewis-Williams, D. 2002. *The Mind in the Cave* (Thames and Hudson)

Lewis-Williams, D. 2005. *Inside the Neolithic Mind* (Thames and Hudson)

McMann, J. 1980. *Riddles of the Stone Age* (Thames and Hudson)

Morris, R.W.B. 1977. *The Prehistoric Rock Art of Argyll* (Poole)

Morris, R.W.B. 1981a. *The Prehistoric Rock Art of Galloway and the Isle of Man* (Poole)

Morris, R.W.B. 1981b. *The Prehistoric Rock Art of Southern Scotland*. BAR Series 86 (Oxford)

Nash, G. and Chippindale, C. (Eds) 2002. *European Landscapes of Rock-Art* (Routledge)

O'Kelly, M. 1982. *Newgrange. Archaeology, Art and Legend* (London. Thames and Hudson)

RCHMS. 1988. *Argyll, Vol. 6.* (Edinburgh: HMSO)

Shee Twohig, E. 1981. *The Megalithic Art of Western Europe* (Oxford)

Shee Twohig, E. and Ronane, M. (Eds) 1993. *Past Perceptions: The prehistoric archaeology of south-west Ireland* (University of Cork Press)

Simpson, J. 1867. *Archaic Sculpturings of Cups, Circles etc upon Stones and rocks in Scotland, England etc and other Countries* (Edinburgh, Edmonston and Douglas)

van Hoek, M.A.M. 1995. *Morris' Prehistoric Rock Art of Galloway* (Oisterwijk, privately printed)

General articles

References to prehistoric rock-art are often scattered, but there are some journals that have recorded new finds and published valuable contributions to Prehistory generally. These include:

The Antiquaries Journal. London (AJ)

Archaeologia Aeliana. Newcastle upon Tyne (AA)

British Archaeology. Council for British Archaeology (CBA)

Cambridge Archaeological Journal (CAJ)

Current Archaeology. London (CA)

Durham Archaeological Journal (DAJ)

Glasgow Archaeological Journal (GAJ)

Northern Archaeology. Northumberland Archaeological Group. Newcastle upon Tyne (NA)

Oxford Journal of Archaeology (OJA)

Proceedings of the Royal Irish Academy

Proceedings of the Society of Antiquaries of Scotland. Edinburgh (PSAS)

Proceedings of the Prehistoric Society (PPS)

Transactions of the Cumberland and Westmorland Antiquarian and Archaeological Society (TCWAAS)

Ulster Journal of Archaeology (UJA)

Yorkshire Archaeological Journal (NAJ)

Some general and specific articles on Prehistoric rock-art include:

Allen, R. 1881. Notes on some un-described stones with cup-markings in Scotland (*PSAS*, XVI)

Armit, I., Dunwell, A.J., Hunter, F.J., McCartney, M. and Nelis, E. 2006. Traprain Law (*CA* 203, 602-7)

Bahn, P., Pettit, P. and Ripoll, S. 2003. Discovery of Palaeolithic cave art in Britain (*Antiquity*, 77, no.296, 227-31)

Barnatt, J. and Reeder, P. 1982. Prehistoric rock art in the Peak District (*Derbyshire Arch. Journal* 102, 33-44)

Barnatt, J. and Robinson, F. 2003. Prehistoric Rock Art in Ashover School and Further New Discoveries elsewhere in the Peak District (*Derbyshire AJ.* Volume 123)

Beckensall, S. 1995. Recent Discovery and Recording of Prehistoric Rock Motifs in the North (*Northern Archaeology* 12. Newcastle)

Beckensall, S. and Frodsham, P. 1998. Questions of Chronology: the case for Bronze Age Rock Art in Northern England (*NA* 15/16. Newcastle)

Beckensall, S. 1997. *Symbols on Stone: the State of the Art* (Council for Independent Archaeology)

Beckensall, S. 1997. Prehistoric Rock Art-Progress and Problems (*At the Edge* No. 8)

Beckensall, S. 1999. Art on the Rocks (*3rd Stone* No. 35)

Beckensall, S. 2004a. 'British Rock Art in 2004' in *The Valcamonica Symposium 2001 and 2002* (National Heritage Board of Sweden)

Beckensall, S. 2004b. 'British Prehistoric Rock Art in 2004' in *The Future of Rock Art – a World Review* (National Heritage Board of Sweden)

Bednarik, R. 2004. 'Millennium: the State of Australian Rock Art Research' in *The Future of Rock Art – a World Review* (National Heritage Board of Sweden)

Bradley, R. 1996. Learning from Places – Topographical Analysis of Northern British Rock Art (*NA* 13/14. Newcastle)

Bradley, R., Harding, J. and Matthews, M. 1993. The Siting of Prehistoric rock art in Galloway, South-West Scotland (*PPS* 59)

Brindley, A. and Killfeather, A. 1993. *Archaeological Inventory of County Carlow* (Dublin: Stationery Office)

Buckley, V. and Sweetman, D. 1991. *Archaeological survey of County Louth* (Dublin: Stationery Office)

Burgess, C. 1990. The chronology of cup and ring marks in Britain and Ireland (*NA*, Newcastle)

Campbell, M. and Sandeman, M. 1964. Mid Argyll: an Archaeological Survey (*PSAS*, XCV 1-125)

Campbell, M., Scott J.G., and Piggott, S. 1960. The Badden Slab (*PSAS*, XCIV)

Campbell, M. 1965. *In Discovery and Excavation in Scotland*

Christison, D. 1903. On the standing stones and cup-marked rocks etc. in the Valley of the Add (*PSAS*, XXXVIII)

Coles, J., Gestdottir, H., and Minnitt, S. 2000. A Bronze Age decorated Cist Cover from Pool Farm, West Harptree: New Analyses (*Somerset Archaeology and Natural History Society*)

Coles, J., 2003. A measure of conviction: recording emphasis in Scandinavian rock carvings (*Antiquity* 77, 297)

Corlett, C. 1999. Rock Art on Drumcoggy Mountain, Co. Mayo (*Journal of Galway Archaeological and Historical Society.* Volume 51)

Cuppage, J. 1986. *Archaeological survey of the Dingle Peninsula* (Ballyferriter: Oidhreeracht Chorca Duibhne)

Craw, J.H. 1929. A Jet necklace from a cist at Poltalloch (*PSAS*, LXIII)

Craw, J.H. 1931. Further Excavations of cairns at Poltalloch (*PSAS*, LXV)

Darvill, T. and Wainwright, G. 2003. A Cup-marked stone from Dan-y-garn, Mynachlog-Dhu, Pembrokeshire, and the Prehistoric Rock-Art from Wales (*PPS* 69, 253-64)

Darvill, T. and O'Connor, B. 2005. The Cronk Yn How Stone and the Rock Art of the Isle of Man (*PPS* 71, 283-331)

Dronfield, J.C. 1995. Subjective Vision and the source of Irish megalithic art (*Antiquity* 69, 539-49)

Dronfield, J.C. 1996. Entering alternative realities: cognition, art and architecture in Irish passage-tombs (*CUJ* 6, 37-72)

Frodsham, P. 1996. Spirals in Time: Morwick Mill and the Spiral Motif in the British Neolithic (*NA* 13/14. Newcastle)

Guilbert, G., Garton, D. and Walters, D. 2006. Prehistoric Cup-and-Ring Art at the Heart of Harthill Moor (*Derbyshire Archaeological Journal*, Volume 125, 12-30)

Hale, A. 2003. Prehistoric rock carvings in Strath Tay (*Tayside and Fife Archaeological Journal*, Volume 9)

Haszeldine, R.N. and Haszeldine, R.S. 2003. Neolithic, natural, or new? Critical observations of cup and ring petroglyphs in Langdale, Cumbria (*TCWAAS*)

Hewitt, I. 1991. *Prehistoric rock motifs in Great Britain* (Unpublished research thesis, Bournemouth University)

Historic Scotland Archaeology Paper. 2003. *Carved Stones: Historic Scotland's Approach* (Historic Scotland)

Johnston, S. 1991. *Distributional Aspects of Irish Petroglyphs* (In Oxbow Monograph 10)

Johnston, S. 1993. The relationship between prehistoric Irish rock art and Irish passage tomb art (*UJA* 12)

Lacy, B. 1983. *Archaeological Survey of County Donegal* (Lifford: Donegal: Donegal County Council)

Mackie, E. and Davis, A. 1989. New light on Neolithic rock carvings: the petroglyphs at Greenland (Auchentorlie) Dumbartonshire (*Glasgow Archaeological Journal* 15)

Morris, R.W.B and Bailey, D.C. 1964. Cup-and-ring marks of SW Scotland (*PSAS*, XCVIII)

Morris, R.W.B. 1967. Cup-and ring marks, part 2 (*PSAS* 100).

Morris, R.W.B. 1970. The Petroglyphs of Achnabreck (*PSAS* 103)

Morris, R.W.B. 1989. The Prehistoric Rock Art of Great Britain: a survey of all sites bearing motifs more complex than simple cup marks (*PPS*, Volume 55).

Nash, G., George, A., Hudson, D., Smith, A. and Stanford, A. 2006. Barclodiad y Gawres – giving up more secrets? (*CA* 2006, 562)

Nowakowski, J. 1991. Trethellan Farm, Newquay: the excavation of a lowland Bronze Age settlement and Iron Age cemetery (*Cornish Archaeology* 30, 5-242)

O'Connor, B. 2003. Recent excavations in a rock art landscape (*Archaeology Ireland*, 17/4, 14-16)

O'Sullivan, M. 1989. A stylistic revolution in the megalithic art of the Boyne valley (*Archaeology Ireland* 3.4)

O'Sullivan, A. and Sheenan, J. 1996. *The Iveragh Peninsular: an archaeological survey of south Kerry* (Cork University Press)

O'Kelley, C. 1973. Passage grave art in the Boyne valley (*PPS* 39, 354-82)

Piggott, S. and Powell, T. 1949. The Excavation of three Neolithic chambered tombs in Galloway (*PSAS* 83, 103-161)

Powell, T. and Daniel, G. 1956. *Barclodiad y Gawres* (Liverpool UP)

Power, D. 1992. *Archaeological inventory of County Cork, 1* (Dublin: Stationery Office)

Ritchie, J.N.G. 1974. Excavation of the stone circle and cairn at Balbirnie, Fife (*AJ* 131, 1-32)

Scott, J. 1989. The stone circles at Temple Wood, Kilmartin, Argyll (*GAJ* 15)

Selkirk, A. 2003. Eogan of Knowth (*Current Archaeology* 188)

Sharples, N. 1984. Excavations at Pierowall quarry, Westray, Orkney (*PSAS* 114, 75-125)

Sherriff, J. 1995. Prehistoric rock-carvings in Angus (*Tayside and Fife Archaeological Journal* 1, 11-22)

Simpson, D. and Thawley, J. 1972. Single Grave Art in Britain (*Scottish Archaeological Forum* 4)

Spratt, D.A. 1982. *Prehistoric and Roman Archaeology of North-East Yorkshire* (BAR 104)

Stevenson, J. 1993. Cup and ring markings at Ballochmyle, Ayrshire (*GAJ* 11)

Stevenson, J. 1997. The Prehistoric Rock Carvings of Argyll, in G. Richie (ed.) *The Archaeology of Argyll*, 95-117 (Edinburgh)

Stewart M. 1958. Strath Tay in the second millennium BC – a field survey (*PSAS* 92, 71-84)

van Hoek, M. 1987. The Prehistoric Rock Art of County Donegal, part 1 (*Ulster Journal of Archaeology*. Volume 50)

van Hoek, M. 1988. The Prehistoric Rock Art of County Donegal, part 2 (*Ulster Journal of Archaeology*. Volume 50)

Waddington, C. 1996. Putting Rock Art to Use. A model of Early Neolithic Transhumance in North Northumberland (*NA* 13/14. Newcastle)

Waddington, C. 1998. Cup and Ring Marks in Context (*CAJ* 8, No.1, 29-54)

Waddington, C. 2005. Excavation of a rock art site at Hunterheugh Grag, Northumberland (*AA Fifth Series*, Volume XXXIV)

The Beckensall Northumberland Archive website (University of Newcastle-Upon-Tyne) is: http//www.rockart.ncl.ac.uk

Index

Places

Achnabreck outcrop (NR855906) 45, 57, 72, 112, 117
Addlebrough cairn 137, 139
Adestie souterrain (NO502344) 170
Airlie souterrain (NO332503) 170
Allan Tofts (NO830030) 154
Anglesey 110, 119
Ardmardock (NR916726) 129
Ardmore stone (Donegal) (C473264) 157
Ardross 129
Arran 40, 92-94, 99
Ashford Primary School (SK347632) 174-5
Aveline's Hole (Somerset cave) 100

Bachwen (SH407495) 121
Badden cist (NR858890) 130
Barbrook barrow (P) 147
Barbrook II stone circle (SK277751) 147
Balblair cairn (NH509447) 124
Baldersdale 87
Ballagawne Keil (I. of Man) 95
Balbirnie (NO285030) 126, 129, 131
Balkemback s/s (NO382384) 124, 158, 159
Ball Cross (SK228691) 147
Ballragh (SC452855) 91
Ballygowan (NO816977) 72
Ballymeanoch s/s (NR933964) 124, 160, 161
Ballyrenan (Tyrone) H373833 121
Ballochmyle (NS512254) 86
Barclodiad y Gawres (SH329707) 120
Barningham Moor (NZ052076) 88
Barnes Lower South s/s (C107245) 158
Barnes Lower North s/s (Donegal) 158

Beanley (N) Location restricted 46, 57
Beltay (Donegal) 157
Ben Lawers 18-22
Beoch cist (NS522809) 126
Bohea stone (L975785) 67, 78
Braes of Taymouth (NN792488) 27
Brittany 61, 110
Brodgar (HY301129) 129
Broomridge (NT973371) 90
Bryn Celli Dhu (SH507702) 119
Blawearie cairns 49, 50, 124-5, 173
Bowes Museum 133
Buttony (NU017310) **colour plate 20**
Byland Moor (SE543806) 140

Cairnbaan (NR838910) 56, 88, 134
Cairnholy (NX517538) 123, 126
Cairn Lath (NC870014) 129
Caerlowrie (NT145745) 129
Calderstones (SD407875) 120
Cardonagh s/s (Donegal) 157
Carn Ban (NR840907) 57, 134
Carlungie souterrain (NO511359) 170
Cartington Cove (NU044091) 98
Castlebar (C. Mayo) 67
Castlerigg (NY292235) 156
Catterline (NO858790) 129
Channel Islands 60, 61
Chapel Stile (NY314058) 69, 75, 77
Chatton Sandyford (NU099272) 125, 133, 154
Clava Cairns (NH757445) 163-7
Clear Island (Kerry) 46
Coilsfield cist (NS446264) 55, 127, 130

People